# A Life of Gratitude

## 21 Days to Overcoming Self-Pity and Negativity

*By Shelley Hitz*

**A Life of Gratitude:** 21 Days to Overcoming Self-Pity and Negativity

Printed in the United States of America
ISBN-13: 978-0615731261
ISBN-10: 0615731260

Join our Facebook group and learn more information at:
www.bodyandsoulpublishing.com/gratitudegroup

# Table of Contents

# Introduction

## The Gratitude Challenge...

**Thankfulness. Gratitude. Contentment.**

These are words that are familiar to us...especially those of us that call ourselves followers of Jesus.

And yet, how often do we get stuck in the opposite...

**Self-Pity. Complaining. Discontentment.**

And I have to admit that I have been there lately. I've been through so many changes recently and some people might think that I have it made. Others might think I'm crazy. But, I don't think many realize how difficult it has been for me.

### The Changes in My Life Over the Last Year

I resigned my job as a Physical Therapist last July to minister and work full time with my husband CJ. This is a dream we have been working towards ever since we came back from being short term missionaries in Belize. When we returned, we had thousands of dollars of debt which (in

1

my thinking) forced me back to my job as a P.T. Although the job is rewarding and pays well, it was not what we felt God called us to in this season. After ministering together and working together for two years in Belize, we sensed that was what we were to continue to do.

However, seven years later, we were finally able to pay off all our consumer debt. Being debt free (except for our mortgage) allowed me to resign my job as a P.T. and embark once again into ministering and working full time together. What a great feeling it was to pay off our debt and yet the transition was harder for me than I anticipated.

I had become dependent on the regular paychecks and benefits that came with my job. And I realized that I got some of my self-worth from my job title. People instantly respected me as a "Physical Therapist" whereas I get very different reactions when I tell someone I am an "Author and Speaker". It's almost as if people want to ask, "Oh really? What's your REAL job?"

God is teaching me to gain my worth from who I am in HIM…not what I do. But, it's been a hard transition.

And then we went from living in a 1300 sq. ft. home to a 125 sq. ft. RV to living in my mom's spare bedroom to finally settling in Colorado Springs in our condo.

What a ride!

I wouldn't go back and do anything different as God used these months of transition in our lives. But, after months of living out of bags and from place to place, I was ready to "nest" again and be settled in ONE place.

When we moved out of our house into our RV, we had to get rid of a lot of stuff. If I would have known that just a few months later we would be moving into a condo in Colorado Springs, I probably would have kept some of the things I gave away. But, the experience taught me a lot about living simply. I realized that I truly didn't "need" all that material stuff. When it really came down to it, I truly only needed a very small amount of material possessions and was able to live without a lot of the stuff I thought I couldn't live without.

When we left Findlay, Ohio, it had been a place I called home for over 20 years. We moved there when I was a junior in high school in 1991 and except for college and our time in Belize, Findlay had been home. All my family lives in Ohio and so to move over 1200 miles away from my "home" was both exciting and sad.

## A Season of New Things in My Life, But Also a Season of Grieving

And here I sit. Although there have been a lot of exciting changes in my life, it's also been a season of grieving.

- Grieving the loss of my job, career and what I thought I would be doing for the rest of my life.
- Grieving the loss of our first house and a lot of the material stuff that filled it.
- Grieving the loss of my "home" for 20 years and living close to my family.

And sometimes we can get stuck in the grief. God has felt distant to me throughout these changes and so sometimes I've felt alone and stuck in self-pity. Poor me. Why can't I live a "normal" life like most people?

## It is Important to Grieve

And so I'm reminded that it is important to grieve...even the little things that don't seem important at the time. My mom always says it is important to feel your feelings and then let them pass, surrendering them into the hands of Jesus so that they don't get stuck or bottled up within us.

And so I have allowed myself to grieve. Even as I've written this post, I've cried a few tears. And for me, many times tears can be healing.

## I Felt Stuck

And yet as I was processing some of my emotions this week I felt stuck. I've given into the habit of working long hours on both ministry and business projects. I believe workaholism is one of my last addictions from which Christ is now working to set me free.

And it's an acceptable addiction in the church and in our culture. It is even often praised.

- Great job, Shelley.
- Wow, you're a real workhorse.
- Look at all you've accomplished.

You get the picture.

It was also my way of trying – in self-sufficiency – to provide financially for our needs. I felt the burden of providing in this way after I quit my P.T. job. I felt the need to replace the income I was giving up when I resigned my job but also wanted to do whatever I needed to do to ensure that I wouldn't need to work a "9 to 5" kind of job again. I wanted to have the freedom to continue to minister with CJ as God opens the doors as well as work from home when, in God's timing, we start a family. We are praying that this happens sooner rather than later, but again trusting God's timing.

Self-sufficiency and workaholism run rampant in our culture, I believe.

It's so easy to get caught up in the rat race. We keep ourselves so busy. Even after resigning my job as a P.T. there were often many times I would work 12 hour days. I am very driven and yet I joked with CJ that I was working harder than I ever did in my P.T. job.

## Praying for Freedom and Contentment

And so here I am. Praying for freedom from the unbalanced life I created. Praying for freedom from the self-sufficiency and workaholism deeply rooted in my life. Praying for contentment in my circumstances.

And then this week I had a friend email me and say she was praying for accountability in a certain area and the only person that came to her mind was me. I agreed to do so for her and asked if she would also help keep me accountable in my workaholism and living a more balanced life. She agreed and I believe God is providing for both of us in this way. Even though we are thousands of miles apart, we are keeping each other accountable via email on a daily basis and praying for each other. God has provided accountability for me in other areas of my life just when I needed it and I believe He is providing it for me again.

## A Reminder of One of Our Greatest Weapons as Christians...a Spirit of Thankfulness and Gratitude

Another thing God kept bringing to my mind this week is thankfulness and gratitude. I was reminded that thankfulness and gratitude are the opposite of self-pity and a complaining spirit.
I know, I know. It seems like a pat answer. "Just be thankful for what you have." "Give thanks in all things." But, there is POWER in being thankful...even when you don't FEEL like being thankful.

I remembered a book I started to read in a Barnes and Noble bookstore one day about a man who began to write thank you notes every day for one year. It wasn't a Christian book but demonstrated the power in being intentionally thankful. I believe it is a Biblical concept that can be experienced by anyone who practices it.

And then I remembered people who I've seen post on Facebook or their blogs something they are thankful for everyday for a series of days. I felt led to do something similar and remembered that...

## It Takes 21 Days to Start a New Habit

Many people say it takes 21 days to start a new habit or break an old one. Whether it is getting in the habit of exercising, eating right or developing a spirit of thankfulness.

And so I decided to take a 21 Day Gratitude Challenge. I hope you'll join me.

However, the gratitude challenge was just my first step. The next step was the 21 prayers of gratitude.

## Prayers of Gratitude

Prayer changes things. It changes me. When I pray consistently to God something changes within me. However, sometimes it is easy to get caught up in the busyness of life and not take the time to pray.

We do not have to pray in a certain way for God to hear us. We can simply lift up the prayer of our hearts to Him as if we are talking with a friend. However, in this book, I have taken key truths from scripture and reworded them into prayers of gratitude. Combining prayer with God's Word is powerful. I have experienced this in my own life and now want to share it with you.

They say it takes 21 days to form a new habit. And so I have shared 21 prayers of gratitude with you to help you form a habit of prayer in your life. I pray that these prayers help you to overcome negativity through applying the power of prayer and God's Word to your life. I also pray that when you finish this book, your prayers will continue on your own. I encourage you to dig into God's Word and come up with your own prayers. If you are struggling in a certain area, I recommend using a concordance or an online tool like BibleGateway.com or BlueLetterBible.org to find scriptures on that topic and then reword them into prayers from your own heart.

*"Pray without ceasing."*
- I Thessalonians 5:17

*"Be anxious for nothing, but in everything by prayer and supplication, with thanksgiving, let Your requests be made known to God; 7 and the peace of God, which surpasses all understanding, will guard Your hearts and minds through Christ Jesus."*
- Philippians 4:6-7

And finally, God led me to compile 21 stories of gratitude to provide encouragement and inspiration.

## Stories of Gratitude

*"If you look at the world, you'll be distressed. If you look within, you'll be depressed. But if you look at Christ, you'll be at rest."*
- Corrie ten Boom

What a great quote by one of my heroes of the faith, Corrie ten Boom. She was a Nazi prison camp survivor and knew what it was like to go through difficult circumstances in life. However, as we share in one of the stories later in this book, Corrie and her sister Betsie found out that it is possible to live life with a grateful heart. They displayed gratitude even when living amongst some of the worst circumstances we can imagine.

How about you? Are you living life to the fullest? Or are you merely surviving from day to day?

One way to live life to the fullest is to live each day with a grateful heart. In this book, we share 21 stories of gratitude to give you encouragement and hope in your own journey. Gratitude is possible! Even though many times we cannot change our circumstances, we can change the way we see them. We can ask God to empower us to change our thoughts. Beth Moore explains this well in a quote from her Patriarchs study, *"I have been told many times, 'Beth, I can't change the way I feel.' But we can change the way we think, which will lead to a change in the way we feel. That's the essences of the renewed mind."*

Our prayer for you is that you find encouragement within these pages. And we pray that you will ask God for His strength to renew your mind with His truth and the hope He offers each one of us every day. It is only through Christ renewing our minds that we can truly live each day with a grateful heart.

*"And do not be conformed to this world, but be transformed by the renewing of your mind, that you may prove what is that good and acceptable and perfect will of God."*
                                                    - Romans 12:2

## Other Resources:

Here are some resources that you might be interested in during this gratitude challenge (and even beyond)...

http://thankfulfor.com - free private or public gratitude journal online

http://itunes.apple.com/us/app/gratitude-journal-for-ipad/id402667476 - $1.99 gratitude journal for iPhone/iPad

https://play.google.com/store/apps/details?id=no.vis tamedia.grattitude - free attitude of gratitude Android app

## Are You Ready to Get Started?

Let's start with a prayer...

*Lord I thank You for each person who will read this book. I pray that You would do a mighty work in their hearts as they spend these next 21 days focused on Your spirit of gratitude in their lives. Change them from the inside out through this challenge, Your Word and prayer. Give them a hunger and thirst for You that will continue past the last page of this book. And replace any negativity and self-pity in their lives with a spirit of gratitude that comes from You. Amen.*

# Day #1

## *21 Days of Gratitude...*

What does this mean?  It can mean different things for different people.  But, for me, I sense that I need to take the initiative to write down the things and people in my life that I am grateful for in my journal for the next 21 days.  At the same time, I will choose one person each day to write a hand-written thank you note to them.  In the note, I will share why I am thankful for them and send it via postal mail.

I found 21 thank you notes and cards in my closet, got them out and wrote my first thank you note today.

Then, I got out my journal – that has been somewhat neglected over the past few months – and wrote out three specific things that I am thankful for in my life today in these three categories: spiritual, physical and relational.  I wrote several sentences of what I am thankful for and why in each category.

And already I can feel the direction of my heart changing.  Imagine what will happen after 21 days of being intentionally thankful for all I've been given.

Because I've been given a lot...more than I deserve.

And it's time to not allow Satan to keep me in the grips of self-pity, a complaining attitude and discontentment. I am asking God to break through in my heart through the power of His Holy Spirit as I take these intentional steps toward gratitude.

## Will You Join Me?

What about you? Will you consider joining me in these 21 Days of Gratitude? It may look different for you and that's okay. Simply ask God what He wants you to do and then do it. It may be as simple as saying out loud one thing you are thankful for each day. Or like me, you may decide to write out thank you notes.

If you feel stuck in self-pity or discontentment, I challenge you to join me. Ask the Holy Spirit to change you as you take simple steps of intentional gratitude in your life. And watch and see what God does.

*"Appreciation is the highest form of prayer, for it acknowledges the presence of good wherever you shine the light of your thankful thoughts."* –Alan Cohen

Psalm 100:4, *"Enter into His gates with thanksgiving, And into His courts with praise. Be thankful to Him, and bless His name."*

## *The Gratitude Challenge:*

~ If you're ready to take this challenge with me and want to share the journey with others, join our private Facebook group here:
www.bodyandsoulpublishing.com/gratitudegroup

Once you are there, I encourage you to post something you are grateful for each day for 21 days. You can also post stories of how God is working in your life through the gratitude challenge.

~ Or buy a notebook and journal and write what you are grateful for each day in it. That's what I did. I chose three categories to write something I'm thankful for each day: spiritual, physical and relational. I also wrote a handwritten thank you card to someone different each day of my 21 days of gratitude challenge.

~ Whatever, you do, I encourage you to spend time focusing on all that God has given you.

## *Prayer of Gratitude:*
## *Grace*

Lord, today I want to thank You for Your grace. Grace is simply getting something good I do not deserve. So many times I take Your grace for granted, please forgive me. Open my eyes to see Your grace more clearly in my life. Lord, I ask that You take the blinders off of my spiritual eyes so that I can see all of the gifts You have so graciously given me.

It is by Your grace ALONE that I am saved from eternal punishment and have the promise that I will be with You in heaven for eternity one day. Thank You for rescuing me from my sin and from the clutches of the evil one, Satan. You died for me so that I could have life and life abundantly. Thank You for Your sacrifice.

Thank You for giving me life each new day. When I wake up in the morning, empower me to focus my first thoughts on You. As I lay my head on the pillow at night, remind me of all that You have given me that day. Show me the gifts You have given me and empower me to say a simple, "Thank You" back to You.

Thank You for Your amazing grace. Without it, I would be in a hopeless situation. But, because of Your grace, I have so much to be thankful for today…and every day.

I love You, Lord. Amen.

*"Every good gift and every perfect gift is from above, and comes down from the Father of lights, with whom there is no variation or shadow of turning."*
                                            - James 1:17

*"For by grace you have been saved through faith, and that not of yourselves; it is the gift of God."*
                                            - Ephesians 2:8

*"The thief does not come except to steal, and to kill, and to destroy. I have come that they may have life, and that they may have it more abundantly."*

- John 10:10

*"May grace (God's favor) and peace (which is perfect well-being, all necessary good, all spiritual prosperity, and freedom from fears and agitating passions and moral conflicts) be multiplied to you in [the full, personal, precise, and correct] knowledge of God and of Jesus our Lord."*

- 2 Peter 1:2 (AMP)

## *Story of Gratitude: Changed From Within*
*Heather Hart*

*"Let the peace of Christ rule in your hearts, since as members of one body you were called to peace. And be thankful."*

- Colossians 3:15 (NIV)

When I first began thinking of a gratitude story to share, I honestly could not think of one. However, after some prayerful contemplation I realized that the reason I could not think of a specific way gratitude has impacted my life, was because it has done so in such a complete way.

You see, several years ago I went through a Revive Our Hearts 30-Day Husband Encouragement Challenge. While I don't remember them ever using the word gratitude to describe what they were teaching us, that is exactly what I

15

got out of it. They encouraged us to not say anything negative to our husbands or about our husbands for 30 days - thus they encouraged us to choose gratitude.

This was in the first years of my marriage. My husband and I were raising four children together, two boys from a previous marriage and our newborn twin girls. As only one of the four was old enough for school, I had to quit my job and become a full time stay at home mommy - there simply were not any jobs that could pay enough to cover the cost of day care for three children - and I was miserable. The only adult I ever saw was my husband. He was coming home from working 12 hour shifts at his job, exhausted, only to encounter a wife that was stressed to the max, and looking for someone to blame and take over. Looking back, I most certainly don't envy what he went through, and have been thanking God ever since for saving my marriage.

Throughout the 30-days of learning to be grateful for my husband, not only did my marriage improve, but my walk with God grew to an entire new level. I started seeing Him in a new way. He wanted me to choose gratitude and thank Him for what He had blessed me with - even when the twins were crying. Even when I hadn't slept for more than an hour at a time in the past 3 months. Even when my husband wasn't reading my mind. Even when the house was a disaster.

Choosing gratitude helped me to see things in a whole new light. It was no longer about where I was, or what was happening in the moment. It was about what I had, and what God had done for me. No, my husband is not perfect, but neither am I. My kids don't always listen, and my house still isn't clean - but God has taught me to be grateful for my life anyway. To be thankful for my wonderful children, and that we have a place to live.

I still have days where the depression sinks in, but God always brings me back to His peace and reminds me of what He has given me. Moreover, even when I'm in the throes of life, I am grateful that my family and my God love me enough to stick with me through it all.

# Day #2

As part of the challenge, I've decided to write a hand-written thank you note each day to someone in my life that I appreciate. Not an email, text or FB message but an actual card that I send in the postal mail. There is something that happens when you write out your thoughts with pen and paper. Plus, it's more meaningful to the receiver because how often do you receive a card in the mail anymore??

*"Nothing is more honorable than a grateful heart."* - Shakespeare

*"I thank my God upon every remembrance of you"*
- Philippians 1:3

## *The Gratitude Challenge:*

I encourage you to send someone you appreciate in your life a hand-written thank you note today. Even if you don't have "cards" to write on, use the paper you have and send a thoughtful note to brighten someone's day!

## *Prayer of Gratitude:*
## *New Beginnings*

Lord, today I want to thank You for new beginnings. Your mercies are new every morning; great is Your faithfulness to me even when I turn my back on You. Sometimes I walk away from You deliberately through sin in my life. But many times, the distance between You and I is a slow fade, where I gradually spend less and less time with You.

And I can feel the difference.

When I spend quality time with You every day, I sense Your presence in my life and Your love, joy and peace. As I get busy and don't intentionally take time to be with You, I can feel a darkness settle over me. It may come in the form of worry, anxiety, self-pity, a complaining spirit or even sin.

Lord, forgive me for the times I have ignored You. You are walking with me each day and yet many times I do not acknowledge Your presence. I am so sorry. Empower me to change through Your Holy Spirit so that I can offer You the best part of my day, every day. Clearly show me how important my time with You is each day and allow me to make You a priority in my life, like I never have before.

Jesus, You knew how important time with Your Father was and often withdrew to a place so that You could be alone with Him. Many times this was early in the morning. Give me the willingness to make sacrifices to spend time with You, even if it means sacrificing sleep or giving up watching my favorite TV show or time on the internet.

I love You, Lord, and thank You for this fresh start today where I can make my relationship with You the biggest priority in my life. Amen.

*"Through the Lord's mercies we are not consumed, Because His compassions fail not. They are new every morning; Great is Your faithfulness."*
                                        - Lamentations 3:22-23

*"I am with you always, even to the end of the age."*
                                        - Matthew 28:20

*"So He Himself often withdrew into the wilderness and prayed."*
                                        - Luke 5:16

*"Immediately He made His disciples get into the boat and go before Him to the other side, to Bethsaida, while He sent the multitude away. And when He had sent them away, He departed to the mountain to pray."*
                                        - Mark 6:45-46


## *Story of Gratitude: Being a "Leperchaun"*
### *Staci Stallings*

A few years ago we had the story of the ten lepers for one of our Vacation Bible School stories. During VBS each year, I write and direct the plays that the teenagers stage for

20

the kids. In the play that year we had ten "lepers"- high schoolers dressed up to look very ill. Some had bandages with red splotches all over them. Some walked with canes, some with crutches.

Most leaned on the kids to walk them to where our Jesus was, moaning, groaning and carrying on the whole way.

It just so happened that day was "crazy hat day" as well. (It's a God thing, trust me!)

Of course if you know the story of the ten lepers, there were ten lepers who were outcasts from society. They went to Jesus to be healed and they were. Jesus then told them to go show themselves to the chief priests at the Temple, which they did.

In the end only one leper thinks to come back and thank Jesus.

Well, as happens so often when God's in charge of things, our "tenth leper" showed up with a very large, very noticeable leprechaun hat. I mean the thing was about 2 feet tall, with a wide brim. It was bright green with darker green vine things that wound up it, and it was velvet.

You could not miss the thing.

Even more so, the leper who was wearing it has a very vivacious personality. He's one of those kids you just notice no matter what he's doing. And he's tall. At the time he was probably close to six-foot, which looks even taller next to first graders. And with that hat, well...

So I want you to picture this. The play started at our church's "west doors." The lepers then "walked" with the kids half-carrying them across the parking lot to the "hut"- a little out building where our Jesus was preaching. This was quite a walk because all the lepers were hanging onto the kids and the kids were trying very hard to carry them and help them get to Jesus.

After this harrowing trip, the lepers all found Jesus and one by one He healed them. They would jump up and yell, "*Yay! I'm healed!*" "*I feel great!*" "*I'm alive!*" And they'd run out of the room.

All ten of them eventually ran out, and Jesus told the kids that through Him and in His Father, there is healing for everyone. In the middle of that speech, who comes running back in but our "Leperchaun"!

Hat still on, he knelt down at the feet of Jesus, which was always, to me such an emotional scene because these two guys in real life were friends. It was always such a reminder of what it will be like when I'm finally there with my friend, Jesus.

The "Leperchaun" was so overwhelmed with gratefulness and said, "*Jesus. Jesus. Thank You so much! I'm healed. I can't believe it. I didn't think it was possible. It's a miracle.*"

Jesus looked down at him and said, "*There were ten. Where are the others? Are you the only one to come back?*"

The "Leperchaun" looked up at Him and said, *"I am, Lord. I am."*

To which Jesus said, *"Stand up and go; your faith has saved you."*

It was a great play.

But it's interesting because in VBS we, as adults, have heard these Bible stories many times, and sometimes we forget that the kids are seeing them for the first time. Even more special, they get to see and hear them right in front of their eyes. Not just hear them in big words they don't understand from the Bible. So they often "get them" in ways that frankly surprise me with their insights and what they get out of it.

Well, at the end of VBS that day, all 150 of the kids were in the gym for the closing ceremonies, and the MC asked what she thought was an easy question, *"How many sick people were there?"* All 150 kids yell, *"TEN!"* And then she said, *"And who was the only one that went back to thank Jesus?"* To which all 150 kids yelled (you guessed it), *"The Leperchaun!"*

The look on her face was absolutely priceless! She wasn't quite sure what to say or to do with that answer - especially because they ALL sounded so sure of it.

God is so funny. He can teach us profound lessons by bringing together little pieces of things we never would have thought to put together ourselves. Every so often, even today nearly six years later, I remember I need to go back and say thanks to Jesus, and I always think, *"Just like the Leperchaun did."* Then I smile because I'm not the only one who remembers that lesson.

The other teens who were helping with the plays that year remember it, my own kids remember, even many of the VBS kids who were there that week remember that "Leperchaun" who remembered to come back and thank Jesus.

So how about you? Are you being a "Leperchaun"? Are you remembering to go back to God and thank Him for what He's done and is doing in your life? Have you thanked Him for the healing, for being there, for loving you?

If not, maybe it's time. Time to be grateful. Time to remember. Time to be a "Leperchaun."

*"Don't worry about anything, but in all your prayers ask God for what you need, always asking him with a thankful heart."* Philippians 4:6 (GNT)

# Day #3

I've started using an outline in my journal as I write out the things I'm thankful for each day in the three categories I've chosen: spiritual, physical and relational. I also make a note of who I wrote a thank you card to that day and why. You can see the outline in the picture here.

As I wrote my thank you note today, I had tears in my eyes. Not tears of sadness but tears of joy and gratitude for all this person has done for me. It was a special moment remembering the many things I have to be thankful for today. I wouldn't have experienced this had I not been purposefully writing out thank you notes to people that I appreciate in my life.

*"You say, 'If I had a little more, I should be satisfied.' You made a mistake. If you are not content with what you have, you would not be satisfied if it were doubled."* - Charles Haddon Spurgeon

*"I know what it is to be in need, and I know what it is to have plenty. I have learned the secret of being content in any and every situation, whether well fed or hungry, whether living in plenty or in want. I can do all this through him who gives me strength."*

- Philippians 4:12-13

## The Gratitude Challenge:

Decide on an outline you want to use and start writing what you are thankful for each day in your journal. If you don't currently have a journal, then I encourage you to start one. It doesn't need to be fancy...many times I have used a 25 cent notebook from Wal-Mart.

## Prayer of Gratitude:
## Unconditional Love

Lord, today I want to thank You for Your unconditional love. Nothing can separate me from Your love and yet many times I do not believe this truth from Your word, the Bible. I struggle to feel and understand Your unconditional love because I don't experience it anywhere else in my life. Others will always let me down or disappoint me at one time or another. No earthly person, aside from You, Jesus, is able to love me perfectly and unconditionally. And sometimes I project my earthly relationships onto You.

However, You are not like any of my other relationships. I can put my full trust in Your love and know that You will always be there for me and love me unconditionally, no matter what I do or what happens to me.

Empower me to grasp how high and deep and wide is Your love for me. Your love is not just a generic love for the entire world, but is also a very personal love directed to me as well. You love me. Let me repeat that to allow that

truth to sink into my mind, heart and soul. You. Love. Me.
And Your love knows no limits, bounds or conditions.
Thank You, Lord, for Your unconditional love for me.
Amen."

*"For I am persuaded that neither death nor life, nor angels
nor principalities nor powers, nor things present nor things
to come, nor height nor depth, nor any other created thing,
shall be able to separate us from the love of God which is
in Christ Jesus our Lord."*

- Romans 8:38-39

*"For this reason I bow my knees to the Father of our Lord
Jesus Christ, from whom the whole family in heaven and
earth is named, that He would grant You, according to the
riches of His glory, to be strengthened with might through
His Spirit in the inner man, that Christ may dwell in Your
hearts through faith; that You, being rooted and grounded
in love, may be able to comprehend with all the saints what
is the width and length and depth and height— to know the
love of Christ which passes knowledge; that You may be
filled with all the fullness of God.*

*Now to Him who is able to do exceedingly abundantly
above all that we ask or think, according to the power that
works in us, to Him be glory in the church by Christ Jesus
to all generations, forever and ever. Amen."*

- Ephesians 3:14-21

## *Story of Gratitude:*
## *Gratitude Saved the Day*

*Gwen Ebner*

A recent visit to Colorado included a camping trip with my daughter, Shelley. We chose Mueller State Park, a picturesque location with a beautiful setting of spruce, fir, pine, and aspen trees, as well as a panoramic view of the Rocky Mountains. I felt excited about camping in view of Pikes Peak even though we were in black bear country. We were reminded of this by the signage advising us of the strict food storage regulations put in place so that we would not tempt bears to come into our site.

We arrived at our campsite and set up the tent. I was eager to have a campfire that evening so we collected firewood. But after taking an invigorating hike in the mountainous area, we returned to our campsite only to encounter raindrops. We decided to sit in the car while waiting for the rainstorm to end. We read, talked, and nibbled on the food we had brought, but as bedtime neared we realized the storm was not going to end anytime soon. So, we decided to retire to the tent for the night.

However, we were not prepared for the heavy rain, wind, hail, and lightning that danced around our tent. We began to feel concern as the rain dripped into our tent and wondered if our small tent was strong enough to withstand the fierce winds of this storm. Should we try to take the tent down in the middle of the night in this heavy storm and head home? I suggested that instead we take turns saying prayers of gratitude. I would pray a few prayers of gratitude and then Shelley would pray. Back and forth we prayed, focusing our mind on God and all the things we were grateful for. And as we did, a peace began to settle over us and we fell asleep. The storm raged most of the night, lasting 12 hours all together. We woke up several times and even slept in the car for a while, but we never again thought of going home because the prayers of gratitude had changed our attitude. Instead of complaining, we began to laugh and see the storm as a new camping adventure!

The storm subsided by morning and we enjoyed lots of hot tea and coffee, along with cereal for our breakfast. We did more hiking and soaked in the beauty of God's creation. We were so grateful that we had not left and missed what God had in store for us that next day. An additional benefit was that instead of taking home a drenched tent that had to be dried, we went home with completely dry camping gear. We learned a wonderful lesson about the power of gratitude...God inhabits the praise of his people and no matter what our situation is we can experience joy!

# Day #4

There are some days that are more difficult to find something to be thankful for in our lives. However, the more we foster an attitude of gratitude the more it gets our focus off of the negativity all around us. As my parents used to always say, "Your glass is either half full or half empty" - it just depends on how you see your life. I'm choosing to see my glass full right now! And it IS changing me. :)

*"We ought to give thanks for all the fortune: if it is 'good,' because it is good, if 'bad' because it works in us patience, humility, and the contempt of this world and the hope of our eternal country." - C.S. Lewis*

*"Be thankful in all circumstances, for this is God's will for you who belong to Christ Jesus."*
                                                      - 1 Thessalonians 5:18 (NLT)

## *The Gratitude Challenge:*

Ask God to help you see the times in your day when you are looking at your life as "half empty" and complaining about the circumstances around you. When you realize this, ask God to help you give that concern to Him in prayer and instead find something to be thankful for at that time. Even if it is something we normally take for granted, like our eyesight or ability to taste food, there is always something to be thankful for in all circumstances.

## *Prayer of Gratitude: The Holy Spirit*

Lord, today I want to thank You for the gift of the Holy Spirit in my life. Jesus, You said You had to go away so that the Helper, the Holy Spirit, would come. And now, because I have put my trust in You, this gift and access to the power of the Holy Spirit has been given to me.

I find it difficult to fully grasp and understand it all, but I thank You for equipping me and giving me the Holy Spirit. The Holy Spirit is my Counselor, Helper and Teacher. The Holy Spirit empowers me with supernatural strength and power to do things that I could not do on my own.

I am so thankful that I am never alone. Jesus, You walk with me, my Heavenly Father is always with me and I am empowered by the Holy Spirit. Thank You, Lord, for providing for me in so many ways.

I am sorry for the times that I have grieved the Holy Spirit in my life and instead have tried to live out of my own strength and power. Please forgive me. Help me to be sensitive to the Holy Spirit and to obey Your promptings in my life. I am so thankful that I do not have to live this life on my own. Thank You for providing what I need today. Amen.

*"Nevertheless I tell you the truth. It is to your advantage that I go away; for if I do not go away, the Helper will not come to you; but if I depart, I will send Him to you. And when He has come, He will convict the world of sin, and of righteousness, and of judgment."*

- John 16:7-8

*"But the Helper, the Holy Spirit, whom the Father will send in My name, He will teach you all things, and bring to your remembrance all things that I said to you."*

- John 14:26

*"But you shall receive power when the Holy Spirit has come upon you; and you shall be witnesses to Me in Jerusalem, and in all Judea and Samaria, and to the end of the earth."*

- Acts 1:8

*"Then Peter said to them, 'Repent, and let every one of you be baptized in the name of Jesus Christ for the remission of sins; and you shall receive the gift of the Holy Spirit.'"*

- Acts 2:38

## Story of Gratitude:
## Gratitude For Every Day
*Suzanne D. Williams*

*"For he hath said, I will never leave thee, nor forsake thee."*

- Hebrews 13:5 (KJV)

I walked out the door today after donning my shoes and tying the laces. I got in my car and drove around town running my errands. Grocery store. Bank. Home improvement center. I gave none of it any thought. Not how I'd get there or what would happen to me along the way. Not who I might meet or when I'd come home.

My daughter went with me. She's my best friend. We joked and chatted about people we know, their funny habits, foibles, and missteps. We let the radio blare, and I smiled as she told me who was singing and recounted all the words.

It was every day, ordinary, boring, and I loved it.

You see, not too long ago my life was the other way around. I stood at the back door, my stomach churning, my fingers numb, and trembled, my mind a mass of confusion. Who am I? Why are we going there again? And mostly, do I have to go?
Home was safe. My spot on the couch was safe. I could sit there and see the same trees, could stick my head out and smell the air, if I had the need, and then withdraw into my sanctuary. Leaving was dangerous. I might fall apart out there. No, I would fall apart out there. I knew it. I would be unable to breathe, unable to think, sick to my stomach.

People would stare at me and shake their heads, saying, *"What is wrong with her?"* They would pull back their children lest they come too close, and I'd find myself once again crumpled on the pavement, nauseous, and wishing some way, somehow, I could go home.

*"Please, just take me home,"* I'd beg my husband. But he would refuse. So I'd count the hours.

I'd tell myself, *"This is just one hour of my time. That's sixty minutes, and the drive adds fifteen. I can do that. Sixty minutes. Oh look, five minutes have passed. Now, it's only fifty-five minutes. I can do fifty-five minutes."* Then forty, thirty-five, thirty, and so on until I arrived back at my secret place.

When the next trip rolled around, I'd do it all over again. It never became easier. I never had some lightning moment when I realized I had done this a thousand times before and so today it was a breeze. Fear never works that way. Instead, I daily leaned on my heavenly Father to hold me up.

Often, I felt his arms beneath me, his feet taking my steps, his breath working in my lungs. He'd whisper in my ear, *"I love you, Suzanne, and you can do this. Just keep walking. Keep relying on me. I'm right here. I will never leave you or forsake you. Never. And that's a long time."*

People look at me today and they see a normal person. I am grateful for that. What they don't see is the miracle Christ worked in my heart. They don't see all the pain it took to get to this place. They don't see the two years before I drove somewhere alone. They don't see the vacation where I got sick halfway there. Or the failed trips to the grocery store. Or that I was afraid to go to church. They don't see me weeping and crying, screaming even, to find peace.

They also don't see the day I sat in my front yard, the green grass filtering through my fingers, a cerulean blue sky overhead, and cast my head back, a smile on my face for the first time in ages, whispering, *"I'm happy. I'm actually happy."*

Gratitude is overlooked in the church. People walk in and walk out. They're focused on hello and goodbye, how are you, and what's for lunch. They want to see what she wore or how he did his hair. Even when the musicians still play, when the girl on the stage has her hands raised in worship, they filter in and out. It's a backdrop - background noise for the other things more important to their day.

But it isn't. Worship is foremost because worship is gratitude. It's me saying, *"Thank you,"* to my Savior for helping me to walk out my door again without any thought, without any consideration, without any fear at all. It's me saying, *"You are holy. You are worthy. You are more than enough."* I know, because I have been there.

# Day #5

To be honest, today was hard for me to complete. I got busy with the day and tasks on hand that I didn't finish my journal entry until the end of the day. For me, it's not about being legalistic about what I do in this challenge (i.e. write a thank you note each day and write in my journal three things I'm thankful for) but about putting Christ first in my life and in my thoughts. Unfortunately, I don't feel like I put Him first today and I could feel the internal struggle all day long.

What God has taught me over and over again is that when I put Him first, everything else will fall into place. Matthew 6:33 says it so perfectly, *"But seek first his kingdom and his righteousness, and all these things will be given to you as well."* (NIV)

And so, today as I asked God for forgiveness for putting other things ahead of Him, I'm also thankful for His forgiveness that washes me as white as snow whenever I confess my sins to Him.

*"Come now, let us settle the matter," says the Lord.*
*"Though your sins are like scarlet, they shall be as white as snow; though they are red as crimson, they shall be like wool."* Isaiah 1:8 (NIV)

## The Gratitude Challenge:

Ask God if there is anything in your heart that is keeping you from an attitude of gratitude. Confess your sin to him and thank him for cleansing you white as snow.

## Prayer of Gratitude:
## Peace

Lord, today I want to thank You for Your peace that passes all understanding. In a world full of stress, anxiety and chaos; I am so thankful for Your peace in my life.

It is so easy for me to give in to feelings of anxiety throughout my day and I ask for Your forgiveness. Empower me to be changed by the renewing of my mind with Your peace and complete trust in You. Just as a young child does not hesitate, but jumps without fear into their father's arms, empower me to trust You fully and to fall into Your capable arms.

Instead of worrying about my circumstances, help me to develop the habit of bringing my concerns to You through prayer. Then, Your peace that passes all understanding will guard and protect my mind and heart.

I would never consider holding on to a grenade where the pin has been pulled and is ready to blow up. Instead, I would throw it as far away from me as possible. In the same way, help me to throw my stress and anxiety onto You. You can handle it…I cannot. When I hold on to my stress, it has the power to destroy me. Right now I visualize myself casting my burdens onto You. I ask You to instead fill me with Your peace through Your Holy Spirit.

Thank You for Your peace that calms my soul. I love You, Lord! Amen.

*"Be anxious for nothing, but in everything by prayer and supplication, with thanksgiving, let your requests be made known to God; and the peace of God, which surpasses all understanding, will guard your hearts and minds through Christ Jesus."*

- Philippians 4:6-7

*"Lean on, trust in, and be confident in the Lord with all your heart and mind and do not rely on your own insight or understanding. In all your ways know, recognize, and acknowledge Him, and He will direct and make straight and plain your paths."*

- Proverbs 3:5-6 (AMP)

*"Casting the whole of your care [all your anxieties, all your worries, all your concerns, once and for all] on Him, for He cares for you affectionately and cares about you watchfully."*

- I Peter 5:7 (AMP)

*"But the fruit of the Spirit is love, joy, peace, longsuffering, kindness, goodness, faithfulness, gentleness, self-control. Against such there is no law."*

- Galatians 5:22-23

## *Story of Gratitude:*
## *Holding On To My Neck*
### *Naty Matos*

When thinking about a story of gratitude in my life it is hard for me to pick just one because my entire life has been an act of gratitude. I have been very blessed. I have encountered many difficult situations throughout my life, but I cannot say *in spite of them*, I instead say *because of them* I am grateful.

I grew up with a single mother who raised me to fear the Lord. He always provided for us and I had many opportunities that others did not have. One of the events in my life that I hold dear as one of gratitude was when I was saved from a car accident. I was in my second year of college and as part of the work/study program I was assisting other students by tutoring those who needed help in language classes. This particular day was a slow one and all the tutors were just hanging out and talking.

For some bizarre reason the conversation turned to what to do when you have a car accident. I had never had one, so I was absorbing the information like a sponge, but had very little to contribute. The one thing that stuck to my mind was the recommendation from one of the guys who said, "*If you're ever in a car accident where your car is hit from behind hold on to your neck to minimize the impact on your neck.*"

After my shift was over I headed home. I was just a left turn away from safely arriving home and as I was waiting to do that left turn a speeding car rear ended me. It all

39

happened so fast, but I quickly realized that I had lost control of my vehicle. I think my spirit left my body for a minute because I have a memory of watching the impact from the sidewalk. The next thing that I remember was placing my hands behind my neck to support my head, not knowing it had been a lifesaving thing to do in that instance.

Once my car stopped moving I was confused for a minute. Some of my neighbors came to my aid, but I was unable to get out of the car. My car was a very small, two door car. The trunk and back seat had been smashed together. The gas tank was underneath my left arm, which was everyone's concern. I'm not sure how long I was stuck inside the car, but it didn't seem long. I do remember the fireman cutting into my car to finally get me out.

I stood up like nothing was wrong. I think it was the adrenaline. But five seconds after my joints stiffened, I couldn't move. I was quickly taken to the hospital, but to their surprise all I had were spasms. Nothing was broken. The doctors told me that because of the force of the impact if I had not held onto my neck I could have broken my neck and died.

God knew I was going to have that accident that day and allowed me to get instructions of what I needed to do to keep myself safe. Many good things came out of what seemed to be a tragic situation. My mother was due to retire two weeks after my accident. She was able to retire the same day of my accident and stay home to take care of me.

This time together at home and during my recovery allowed us to bond in a way that we never could previously while she was working and I was in school.

Some days I still struggle with the effects of that accident. I have days where my neck stiffens more than others or my back locks up and I have to lay low for a few days. But considering the magnitude of the accident, I live a normal life that has not hindered me. I live a life of gratitude and do things like rock climbing, hiking and other mini adventures that I have challenged myself to do. I am very grateful that God saved my life that day. I am grateful that He prepared me for what was coming and that I recovered quickly and almost completely.

If I was to write all the things that I am grateful for, I would have to write a book that included every second of my life, without leaving any of them out. I am grateful for every tear because it has brought me closer to God, every moment of laughter because I have enjoyed it, every annoyance because it has helped me grow, even every day of laziness because I have truly enjoyed doing nothing on those rare occasions I get to do so.

If I had to answer this question some years before I may had given a different answer, but once I had the revelation that I am nothing, that I have nothing and that all I am belongs to HIM. I am grateful for every breath of air that I am given because it is a gift.

# Day #6

As I was writing a thank you card today, I was thinking about some good reasons to send a thank you card. There are many reasons but here are just a few...

1. Thank someone for a gift they gave you (Christmas, birthday, etc)
2. Thank someone for something they did for you (i.e. watched your kids while you were at a meeting, mowed your lawn, brought you food etc.)
3. Thank someone for hosting you at their home (for dinner, overnight, etc.)
4. Thank someone for brightening your day (i.e. salesperson who was exceptionally helpful, co-worker that encouraged you, etc.)
5. Thank someone for being in your life. This is a great opportunity to thank those we take most for granted. (i.e. husband/wife, mother/father, siblings, children, etc.)

Those are just a few ideas to get you started. I'm sure you can think of many more!

*"If we pause to think, we'll have cause to thank."* –Selected

*"We give thanks to the God and Father of our Lord Jesus Christ, praying always for you, 4 since we heard of your faith in Christ Jesus and of your love for all the saints."*
- Colossians 1:3-4

## *The Gratitude Challenge:*

What are some other reasons you can think of for sending thank you cards? Write out at least two more reasons of your own and then send a thank you card to someone in your life.

## *Prayer of Gratitude: Guidance and Direction*

Lord, today I want to thank You for the guidance and direction You give me every day through the Holy Spirit. Sometimes I wander off Your path and start doing what I think it best without consulting You. Please forgive me for making decisions apart from You. Empower me to change and put You at the center of everything I do.

You have promised to never leave me nor forsake me. You are with me every step of the way, every single day. When I am at a crossroads and do not know what to do, remind me to come to You first, even before my family and friends. Your guidance and direction is what I want more than anything else.

I am so thankful that You instruct me and teach me in the way I should go. I have experienced the promptings of the

Holy Spirit that guide me and I know that You have my best interests in mind, even when the path gets difficult. You also guide me through Your word, the Bible. It is a lamp unto my feet and a light unto my path.

When I get stuck and don't know what to do, all I need to do is simply pray and ask You. You have promised to give me wisdom when I ask You for it. Thank You, Lord, for the way You lovingly lead and guide me each day. Open my ears so that I can hear Your still, small voice. Amen.

*"I will never leave you nor forsake you."*
                                                                    - Hebrews 13:5b

*"I will instruct you and teach you in the way you should go; I will counsel you with my loving eye on you."*
                                                                    - Psalm 32:8 (NIV)

*"Your word is a lamp to my feet and a light to my path."*
                                                                    - Psalm 119:105

*"Whether you turn to the right or to the left, your ears will hear a voice behind You, saying, 'This is the way; walk in it.'"*
                                                                    - Isaiah 30:21 (NIV)

*"If any of you lacks wisdom, let him ask of God, who gives to all liberally and without reproach, and it will be given to him. But let him ask in faith, with no doubting, for he who doubts is like a wave of the sea driven and tossed by the wind."*
                                                                    - James 1:5-6

# Story of Gratitude:
## From Sorrow to Joy
### *Janet Perez Eckles*

*This story of gratitude was originally shared by Janet in an audio interview as part of the "Unshackled and Free" online conference and transcribed. You can get access to the entire interview here: http://theforgivenessformula.com/conference

God has turned my sorrow into joy. What sorrow? Well, I have walked through losing my sight at age 31, dealing with marital infidelity and also losing my youngest son to murder. For those that are grieving, dealing with anger or unforgiveness or struggling with self-pity the most practical advice I would give you is to learn to accept God's ways. Obviously, if you are still in the middle of the emotions, you are still trying to resolve it and find healing in your own way. You have to make a decision to say, *"Yes, Lord, from now on it's not going to be me anymore, it's going to be you and it's going to be your ways."*

It is also important to be committed to read His Word. I can read one verse of the Bible and you can read the very same verse, but it can speak differently to each of us. This happens because they aren't just words on a piece a paper but God's anointed message to each of us with the power that it carries.

Also, when you wake up each day your thinking needs to be turned toward gratitude. My husband, Gene, and I have one program we watch all the time. One of the pastors said you need to wake up and find a way to always be grateful...to be grateful for what you have. You need to be appreciative. And he said that there may be someone thinking, "Yes, you have a lot to be grateful for. Look at how you have this mega church, you have people helping you, you have a vibrant ministry, your health is intact and you have your family. Of course, you can be grateful but what about me? What about me? I just lost my home. My husband is out of a job for years and what do I have to be grateful for?'

So, this pastor replied, "What I would say to that person is that an attitude of gratitude is one that I wake up and choose every morning and gives me a different perspective. Yes, I could get up in the morning and begin saying 'Oh, poor me. I don't know how I'm going to make it to the bathroom. I can't even see my way out of the bedroom.' But, instead, I say 'Thank you, Lord, that you have given me ears, that you have given me eyes of the heart to see. I can walk. I can talk. I can do so many things. I want to thank you for that and I want to say thank you for what you will do for me today.' I believe that everyone without an exception has something to be grateful for and something to say, 'Lord, this is what I appreciate and I'm going to focus on that and I'm going to praise you because you deserve the thanks.'"

So, an attitude of gratitude has to be foremost on our mind. Our thinking can be so powerful.

So often when I have so many tasks to do with the ministry, and working full-time, and traveling, and preparing, I could begin to think, "Oh, if I could only see I could do so much more." Or "Oh, goodness, if I could only see I could get to this website," or "If I could only have my son back, if I didn't have to…" All that negative thinking would already defeat me. It would change my attitude. It could even affect my health, so I always choose to think "Lord, I am so grateful. Yes, I have a glitch. My screen reader stopped talking." A glitch like that is similar to a sighted person looking at a blank screen. Instead I say, "Ok, Lord, you want me to say something else" and I begin to repeat a verse. Controlling our thinking is so important.

As the Bible says, *"Whatever is true, whatever is noble, whatever is right, whatever is pure, whatever is lovely, whatever is admirable – if anything is excellent or praiseworthy, think about such things."* Philippians 4:8 (NIV). Because the minute we think, *"Well I'm not going to think negative. I'm not going to…"* Just like if you look at a piece of chocolate cake and say, *"I'm not going to eat it, I'm not going to eat. I don't want any more."* Guess what you're going to do? You are going to want to eat it even more. So, I encourage you not to think of what you don't want to do. Think of something else. So, I always think of the positives; the good, the lovely, the right, the excellent and, of course, we always have the Lord to think about. This will then change your thinking.

Now, I don't want you to think that right now my life is perfect. There are issues in my life right now that are extremely difficult and I don't know how the Lord is going to resolve them. My oldest son has recently learned he has the same disease I do and he is also starting to lose his sight. So, you see, there's another issue that could get me down.

47

None of us can expect the Christian life to be perfect, but we have a perfect God who says, "You know what? I always knew this was happening. This doesn't catch me by surprise. Didn't I promise you that I overcame the world? I overcame. I triumphed over that. Will you come with me to show you how I'm going to triumph over this too?'"

*"I have told you these things, so that in me you may have peace. In this world you will have trouble. But take heart! I have overcome the world."*

– John 16:33 (NIV)

# Day #7:

It's hard to believe it's been a week since I first started this challenge. One week down, two to go. :) And I'm realizing more than ever that what Henri Nouwen says in the quote below is so true...

*"Gratitude...goes beyond the 'mine' and 'thine' and claims the truth that all of life is a pure gift. In the past I always thought of gratitude as a spontaneous response to the awareness of gifts received, but now I realize that gratitude can also be lived as a discipline. The discipline of gratitude is the explicit effort to acknowledge that all I am and have is given to me as a gift of love a gift to be celebrated with joy."* - Henri J.M. Nouwen

*"And we also thank God continually because, when you received the word of God, which you heard from us, you accepted it not as a human word, but as it actually is, the word of God, which is indeed at work in you who believe."*
- I Thessalonians 2:13

## *The Gratitude Challenge:*

Look up the word thanks and thanksgiving in the Bible using a concordance or www.biblegateway.com. Then, choose one verse to memorize.

## *Prayer of Gratitude: Nature*

Lord, today I thank You for the beauty of Your creation, nature. Your beauty surrounds me every day and I am reminded of You. Thank You for these simple gifts to enjoy each day.

* Flowers
* Sunsets
* Rivers
* Mountains
* Rainbows

And the list could go on and on. The beauty of Your creation amazes me and reminds me of Your creativity. Thank You for allowing me to enjoy Your creation each day no matter where I am. Whether I am walking along the beach, on a trail in a forest or along the sidewalk of a busy city – Your fingerprints are all around me.

I love the smells of nature as well: the fragrance after the rain, the sweetness of fresh flowers or the scent of pine trees.

May I never take Your creation for granted and thank You for the beauty You surround me with each day.

*"The heavens declare the glory of God; the skies proclaim the work of his hands."*

- Psalm 19:1

*"The earth is the Lord's, and all its fullness, the world and those who dwell therein. For He has founded it upon the seas, and established it upon the waters."*

- Psalm 24:1-2

*"For by Him all things were created that are in heaven and that are on earth, visible and invisible, whether thrones or dominions or principalities or powers. All things were created through Him and for Him."*

- Colossians 1:16

## *Story of Gratitude:*
## *A Card For Gratitude*

*Lorilyn Roberts*

Can we give thanks in all things? There is a time I would have said no. I used to ask with the wrong attitude, why didn't God take care of this? Why did He allow that to happen? I felt smug in my self-righteousness. After all, I was a victim in many situations - receiving injustice when I didn't deserve it. If God really loved me, He would fix this or solve that, unless He abandoned me, too. A thankless heart grieves the Holy Spirit, hurting not only our relationship with God, but also others. We feel it in our emotions - bitterness, anger, and depression.

Gratitude is a strange gift. The more we are thankful, the more we remember things for which we are thankful. One of my most memorable moments of gratitude came when I was in the eighth grade. I lost my notes for a major term paper. I didn't know the cards were missing until my final class and the bell rang to be dismissed. I panicked. I ran down the hall into one class after another, checking my desk for the missing notes. Each time when they weren't there, more tears filled my eyes. The dozens of hours of work I had put into those cards flashed before me and redoing all that work sickened me. In the last desk I checked, I found my stack of notecards.

I wrapped my arms around them and smiled, thanking God for helping me to find them. Tears flowed - not tears of sadness but tears of joy. I was a straight "A" student and the thought of those cards being lost forever was enough to send me into a tailspin of deep depression.

Recently I got to thinking about those cards. Much has happened since that day almost forty years ago. Now that I am a little older and a little grayer, I have accumulated many notes - for a different kind of term paper. We are living notes for God's Book of Remembrance. Some of those notes I didn't want to write and would gladly have thrown them away. They were about topics I never would have chosen, but God had different plans.

My notecards have included lessons in disappointment, heartache, failure, worry, depression, fear, and insecurity. Why couldn't God have given me easier topics like how to live like a millionaire? I would have donated lots of money. I could handle that one. As the years have passed and they go by faster the older I get, missing from some of those cards written long ago was one important word - gratitude. Did I really want to thank God for the husband who abandoned me and married his pregnant girlfriend? Did I really want to thank God for my barrenness? Did I really want to thank God for the twenty years I spent in a profession I hated?

God has taken me down many paths I didn't like. During most of those years, I did not have a heart of gratitude. I needed to learn, before God could use me completely, I needed to surrender to Him completely. Anything we hold back in our lives and put before God is an idol. God can't use us as He would like to if we don't surrender all to Him in obedience. Otherwise, we will not be able glorify Him fully but we will be too busy seeking our own selfish ambitions. We may not even realize it or do it intentionally.

Look at Hollywood, scan the self-help books, listen to the news, read the top stories on the internet - what blessings can the world give us with its self-centered, "I" focused mentality? If I had continued to be like the world, which I was drawn to, I never could have glorified God, and you wouldn't receive a blessing for God's work in me.

I am thankful God didn't give me all that I wanted when I was young. I would still be an insecure, fearful, performance-driven individual, seeking my self-worth from the world. How could God use me with that kind of mindset? The hard things God put in my life did a great work once I surrendered to Him. He humbled me and showed me His omnipotent power and infinite wisdom.

I cringe when I think of what kind of a mother I would have been to my kids if God had given me children when I was married - a co-dependent, insecure wife seeking all her self-worth from her husband. Talk about dysfunctional in today's psychological terms. I was clueless what it meant to be a Christian wife or a Christian mother.

Today I thank God for the divorce that brought me to my knees. I honestly think I loved my husband more than I loved God. I just didn't know it. I recommitted my life to Jesus Christ and God became my husband and my provider.

Growing up in a single-parent family without a father was hard. Being fatherless opened the door for my stepfather to adopt me when I was ten. His adoption of me paved the way for a deeper understanding of what it means to be adopted by my heavenly Father.

My barrenness became a blessing as I adopted two beautiful daughters from Asia. And the only one who loves them more than I do is God Himself.

I could never see the value of my job as a court reporter. How would God ever use all of those words I wrote involving lawsuits that had no lasting or eternal value? Why didn't God allow me to pursue my dreams of becoming an author? Did He not put those dreams in my heart? Only when I prayed to God to make me more thankful for the job I hated did God give me something more fulfilling. Those court-reporting skills gave me the foundation for a later career in broadcast captioning, allowing me to work from home while raising my two adopted daughters. Now that I have time to write, I can pursue the passion to write God gave me, but in His timing, not mine.

When I was young, I looked at the destination, not the process, but it is in the process we grow and become like God. If the process had no meaning, God could have snapped His fingers and made us perfect right away. Wouldn't that have been much more efficient and saved a lot of time? But God didn't want to do it that way.

Why? It's in the process that we glorify God. What is more beautiful than to see a man or a woman who has overcome great adversity give praise to Jesus Christ? We've all seen it and we stand amazed. How easy it is to forget God's passion. He sacrificed His Only Begotten Son, Jesus Christ, so why would God withhold anything good from us? There is a mystery in it, but at the center is God. The joy is in the journey itself and all the opportunities He gives us along the way to glorify Him.

If our attitude towards the hard things glorifies God, we will be fulfilled. As Paul says in Philippians 4:13, "*I can do all things through Christ who strengthens me.*" (KJV) In the end, we are most content when we're filled with God because our true joy can only be found in Him-not in this world. Everything else not of God will fade away and soon be forgotten.

It is in the struggle and my inability to do anything without God that I see His power at work. I am as a helpless worm, but God comes alongside and lifts me up when I fall. More than once, He has sent friends to me when I needed encouragement. Scripture instructs me each day, and prayer draws me into sweet communion.

When I enter heaven's gates, God will wipe away my tears. Until then, I will write, hoping to use those cards of suffering to point people to the One who is the Source of all Hope and the Giver of all Joy. The cross is my symbol of remembrance. If I had not given my "all" to God, I never would have seen redemption in the hard things. Perspective is everything. God never wastes anything.

As it says in  Philippians 4:8, "...*Whatsoever things are true, whatsoever things are honest, whatsoever things are just, whatsoever things are pure, whatsoever things are lovely, whatsoever things are of good report; if there be any virtue, and if there be any praise, think on these things.*" (KJV)

Only through God's grace could I find hope when I had no hope. Thankfully, God never gave up on me even though I tried to give up on myself. He changed my perspective, showed me his unconditional love, and helped me to be thankful for even those things I hated. God lessened my pain and brought Godly friends into my life. In Jesus I found freedom to love and forgive. With a grateful heart, I found God at work in all those things I once despised, and for that, I am thankful.

# Day #8:

Yesterday was hard and I felt myself sinking into self-pity. All my efforts to try to find something to be thankful for fell short because I was trying to fight a spiritual battle in my own strength. It wasn't until we attended a church service last night that I began to feel a breakthrough. I cried almost the entire time during the worship as the Holy Spirit ministered to me. I still have to fight the battle each day but God reminded me that He has given us the victory over any darkness that threatens to overtake us through Jesus Christ.

*"But thanks be to God, who gives us the victory through our Lord Jesus Christ."*

- 1 Corinthians 15:57

*"Gratitude is the least of the virtues, but ingratitude is the worst of vices."* - Thomas Fuller

## The Gratitude Challenge:

Thank Jesus today for the victory he has given you over self-pity and an ungrateful, complaining spirit. Ask for the empowerment of His Spirit to help you overcome any darkness that threatens you today.

## Prayer of Gratitude:
## *Hope*

Lord, today I thank You for the hope I have in You. This life is not all there is and for that I am so thankful. Many people live for this life only; however, I know that there is so much more. Thank You that the best is yet to come in heaven.

Even though the hard days hit and dark times come on this side of heaven, I know that I can still hope. The enemy wants me to feel as if I am trapped inside a dark room without any doors to escape. However, You remind me that I am not trapped in a room, but simply walking through a tunnel. This too shall pass. Thank You for walking with me through the dark days and giving me hope even when I can't see the end.

Thank You for the hope of heaven. I look forward to seeing You face to face and being in a place where there will no longer be tears or pain. What a day it will be.
Your hope sustains me, Lord. Thank You for strengthening me with Your hope today. I love You. Amen.

*"We give thanks to the God and Father of our Lord Jesus Christ, praying always for you, since we heard of your faith in Christ Jesus and of your love for all the saints; because of the hope which is laid up for you in heaven, of which you heard before in the word of the truth of the gospel."*
                                                    - Colossians 1:3-5

*"Now may the God of hope fill you with all joy and peace in believing, that you may abound in hope by the power of the Holy Spirit."*

- Romans 15:13

*"Blessed is the man who trusts in the Lord, and whose hope is the Lord,"*

- Jeremiah 17:7

*"Let us hold fast the confession of our hope without wavering, for He who promised is faithful."*

- Hebrews 10:23

## Story of Gratitude: Cherished Memories

*Alberta Sequeira*

People will probably wonder how I can write about gratitude when I lost my husband, Richie and my daughter, Lori, from their alcohol addiction. The word means thankfulness, grateful and appreciation. How can I feel gratitude, especially after losing a child?

First, we have to come to the realization that we all belong to God and each one of us is a gift to another person. We are only here on earth for a short period of time. It's what we did with that person while they were with us that count.

I took my loved ones for granted because I never expected God to call them home early. I thought that there was a bubble that surrounded me and I was protected from that kind of tragedy.

59

Anyone coming from an alcoholic family life knows that it's an existence with fear, confusion and abuse. Family members suffer in silence behind closed doors. It's very hard for any sibling including the addicted to open up with our emotions. We bury our needs deep down inside us.

I have the blessing of knowing that God is all loving and merciful. I will never find the answers to why Richie and Lori didn't fight harder for their recovery. I have to trust that God had a reason for taking them home.

My gratitude is from being chosen to reach out to other substance abusers to help them see the danger of going down the same path fighting their usage and staying in denial.

I'm thankful that God had sent me my daughter, Lori, for thirty-nine years. She brought me joy with her laughter and love of family and life itself. Lori left me a granddaughter, Meagan, who is now going for her Master's Degree in Psychology so she can treat people with alcohol, drug and mental health problems. Her son, Joe, is a Marine who is due to get out of the service next year. Lori would have been very proud of them.

We can stay curled up in a ball and never move forward from a death or we can take our agony and help others. I wrote my two memoirs so I could share my mistakes and my private talks that I give to patients on "The Effect of Alcoholism on the Whole Family" and with readers who can learn from my wrong choices. If Richie and Lori had lived, I would not have become an Awareness Coach who is on a journey to help people realize that it's not that alcohol abuse may, would or could kill. It will.

Appreciation is about sharing my life with others who are traveling down the same path as mine. I value my other daughter, Debbie, who also gave me a grandson, Michael and a granddaughter, Kerri. She lost her only sibling.

In 1993, I married my husband, Al, sold my home and moved into his located in Rochester, Massachusetts. It's a small town with rolling farmland and beautiful country scenery. I have two step-daughters and two-step sons who are my children. With our two combined families, Al and I are blessed with ten grandchildren from the youngest being six and the oldest who is twenty-four years old.

Alcoholism is a disease that is out of control around the whole world. Gratitude is also described as "a sense of obligation." I feel obligated to help alcoholics even if it's just one person who gets strength from me. I plant the seed of hope for them to recover and put the rest in God's hands because I have done His work.

# Day #9:

Today is Memorial day and so I wrote a thank you note to my Grandpa ("PawPaw") who is now 96 and served in the army in WWII. And I'm so thankful that God preserved his life as I would not be here otherwise.

*"Thanksgiving is a recognition of a debt that cannot be paid. We express thanks, whether or not we are able otherwise to reimburse the giver. When thanksgiving is filled with true meaning and is not just the formality of a polite 'thank you,' it is the recognition of dependence."* - Billy Graham

*"So we, Your people and sheep of Your pasture, Will give You thanks forever; We will show forth Your praise to all generations."*

- Psalm 79:13

## The Gratitude Challenge:

Send a thank you note to someone you know that has served or is serving in the military.

## Prayer of Gratitude:
### Strength

Lord, today I thank You for the strength You give me. I feel weak and fragile today - and yet I know that when I am weak, You are strong. Infuse me with Your strength today.

Just as my cell phone needs recharged regularly, I need recharged as well. My recharging comes from spending time with You and I thank You that it can even be as simple as saying two words - "Jesus, help." You long to give me strength and to recharge me physically, emotionally and spiritually. Remind me often throughout my day of Your presence with me.

Lord, apart from You I can do nothing. And I feel it. When I try to do things in my own strength I get tired and overwhelmed very easily. But, when I am depending on Your strength, I can run and not grow weary. Thank You for giving me the strength I need to face whatever comes my way today. I love You. Amen.

*"Therefore I take pleasure in infirmities, in reproaches, in needs, in persecutions, in distresses, for Christ's sake. For when I am weak, then I am strong."*

-2 Corinthians 12:10

*"I am the vine; you are the branches. If you remain in me and I in you, you will bear much fruit; apart from me you can do nothing."*

- John 15:5 (NIV)

63

*"But those who wait on the Lord shall renew their strength; They shall mount up with wings like eagles, they shall run and not be weary, they shall walk and not faint."*
- Isaiah 40:31

## Story of Gratitude:
## God's Protection and Healing
*Lucille Richardson*

When I was 29 years old, our family moved to a new house in Carlisle, Ohio. Soon after, on a Saturday, I decided to go and buy some new window treatments for our house. In those days the stores closed at 6:00 pm and did not reopen until Monday morning.

My husband Arthur and I had three daughters: Robyn, who was six months old, Gwen, five years old, and Donna seven years old. Gwen decided to go along with me to the store and I left the other girls with Art. The store was about a mile from our house and I had left the house at 4:30 pm.

Around halfway through the trip I went around a curve, but was driving too fast, being in a hurry to get there before the store closed. I tried to slow down but spun instead, heading down toward the river. Instead of ending up in the river, I hit a tree and the motor was knocked up into the front of my car. My head hit the windshield and I got cut pretty badly and I was pinned in the car by the stirring wheel.

I realized I was not going to be able to get out myself. However, I saw a car down the road with a man fixing a flat tire. I laid my body on the horn and the sound brought

64

him to see about me. He saw that he couldn't get me out either, so he called 911 from a nearby farm house. The ambulance came and had to use a blow torch to get me out. On the way to the hospital in the ambulance, my daughter, Gwen, kept saying, *"Mommy, are you going to be all right; you're hurt"*. I still didn't realize how badly I was hurt and reassured her I would be okay.

Since this was Saturday night, the hospital had to call a doctor at his home to come in and see me. I ended up in shock for two days and ended up with a broken hip and ankle. My ankle was broken so badly that it was hanging on by a piece of skin. It turned black and wouldn't stop bleeding.

When I came out of shock, I could hear two doctors saying, *"It looks like we will have to take her foot off; it doesn't want to stop bleeding."* I had such a huge need for blood that almost everybody on our street donated some blood for me. My dear mother, Catherine, came to take care of our girls and called the "Prayer Chain" at church. In the Middletown area there are eight Churches of God and they started praying for me. After that, I heard the doctors say, *"Something has happened; the blood has stopped."* To this day, I am a firm believer that it was God's healing power that saved my life. I ended up staying in the hospital for a month.

A short time later, I was at a family gathering and fell while I was using crutches. The pin that was in my hip had to be taken out and skin had to be grafted on my ankle. I was in the hospital again for two more weeks.

During my time in the hospital I was reminded that my husband's mother had died when he was two years old, leaving him without a mother. So I asked the Lord to let me live long enough to raise my girls. I am deeply grateful that God honored my prayer. My girls are now grown and have children and grandchildren of their own. So, I suppose you might say that I am living on borrowed time. And in addition, I am grateful that my daughter, Gwen, was not hurt and only in the hospital overnight.

I give all the glory to God for my healing and have deep gratitude to all the people who prayed for me. I praise the Lord for His healing power!

# Day #10:

Corrie ten Boom is one of my hero's and role models in this life. She was a Nazi camp survivor that God used in amazing ways through her writing and speaking as she traveled around the world. As I was reading in her book, "Amazing Love" this morning, this quote impacted me. So many times the things we complain about are things that God has already given us. We just need to come to him and "cash the check" He has already given us. I encourage you to read Corrie's analogy and then ask God how He wants you to apply it to your life today.

*"The Bible is a checkbook. When you said yes to Jesus Christ, many promises were deposited to your credit at that very moment, and they were signed by the Lord Jesus Himself. But now you have to cash your checks in order to profit by them. When you come upon such a promise and say, 'Thank you, Lord, I accept this,' then you have cashed a check, and that very day you'll be richer than you were the day before."* - Corrie ten Boom

*"Blessed be the God and Father of our Lord Jesus Christ, who has blessed us with every spiritual blessing in the heavenly places in Christ"*

- Ephesians 1:3 (NKJV)

## *The Gratitude Challenge:*

Write out at least 5 spiritual blessings you have been given through Christ. Thank Him for those blessings today by saying, "Thank you Lord, I accept this."

## *Prayer of Gratitude:*
## *Protection*

Lord, today I want to thank You for Your protection over my life. I thank You that when I put my trust in You, You will be my shield and my refuge. You are my hiding place and protect me from trouble.

There is evil all around me and I can feel the spiritual battle every day. And yet, You are my protector and You shield me from the enemy. This does not mean that I will never experience trouble in this life, but it does mean that You will be with me and that in the end You will overcome. You are a strong tower and when I run to You, Jesus, I am safe.

I claim Your promise today that says "no weapon formed against me shall prosper." I command any evil spirits to leave me in Jesus name and thank You for the blood of Jesus that covers me and protects me from the evil one. Thank You for Your protection over me physically, emotionally and spiritually today. Amen.

*"You are my hiding place; You shall preserve me from trouble; You shall surround me with songs of deliverance."*
                                                                    - Psalm 32:7

*"The name of the Lord is a strong tower; the righteous run to it and are safe."*

- Proverbs 18:10

*"No weapon formed against you shall prosper, and every tongue which rises against you in judgment you shall condemn. This is the heritage of the servants of the Lord, and their righteousness is from Me," says the Lord."*

- Isaiah 54:17

*"But the Lord is faithful, and he will strengthen you and protect you from the evil one."*

- 2 Thessalonians 3:3 (NIV)

*See also Psalm 91.

## Story of Gratitude:
## Giving Thanks for the Littlest Things... Even Fleas
*CJ Hitz*

Many of us could say that we've had heroes we looked up to. Some of these heroes are still alive and others have long passed away. For Shelley and I, Corrie ten Boom is one such person. Though she died in 1983, Corrie continues to be an inspiration through her many writings that remain as relevant as ever. We sometimes refer to her affectionately as "Granny" because of the influence she's had on us in our walk with Jesus and the fact that she lived to be 91 years old.

Corrie and her family were arrested in 1944 for helping many Jews hide and escape the Nazi Holocaust during World War II. She and her sister Betsie would eventually be sent to the Ravensbruck concentration camp, where Betsie died. Like millions of others sent to these horrific facilities, Corrie and Betsie endured humiliation, ridicule, disease, hunger and cold in the 9 months they were imprisoned.

Corrie and Betsie were fortunate enough to remain together even though they were separated from other family members who were arrested. Corrie was constantly referring to Betsie's strength, perseverance and faith in the midst of the most depressing conditions. But it was perhaps Betsie's spirit of gratitude that spoke loudest to Corrie and those who knew her.

One such instance of gratitude occurred after they were transferred to permanent quarters known as Barracks 28. Upon being ushered through the door by a guide, they encountered broken windows and an overwhelming smell that told them the plumbing had most likely backed up. They also noticed the bedding had been soiled and was rancid. Speaking of beds, they were stacked three high and wedged so close together, there was hardly an aisle to walk between these bare wooden structures.

As they laid down that first night on the rancid-smelling straw which served as bedding, fighting back waves of nausea, Corrie felt something pinch her leg.

*"Fleas! Betsie, the place is swarming with them!"*

As they scrambled out of the bed they shared, they continued to feel the tiny pests biting them...

*"Here! And another one!"* Corrie wailed. *"Betsie, how can we live in such a place!"*

Betsie began to pray and ask the Lord to show them how they could live in such misery. Before she finished, she sensed the Lord's answer in the words of the bible passage they had read earlier that morning...

*"Encourage the fainthearted, help the weak, be patient with them all. See that no one repays anyone evil for evil, but always seek to do good to one another and to everyone. Rejoice always, pray without ceasing, give thanks in all circumstances; for this is the will of God in Christ Jesus for you."* – 1 Thessalonians 5:14-18 (ESV)

*"That's it, Corrie! That's His answer. 'Give thanks in all circumstances! We can start right now to thank God for every single thing about this new barracks!"*

Corrie then responded, *"Such as?"*

Betsie then began to name some things...

*"Such as being assigned here together."*
*"Such as the Bible in your hands."*
*"Thank you Lord for the crowding in here which will allow so many to hear what's read in these pages."*
*"Thank you Lord for the fleas."*

When Betsie mentioned the fleas, Corrie responded, *"The fleas! Betsie, there's no way even God can make me grateful for a flea."*

*"Give thanks in all circumstances"*, Betsie quoted. *"Fleas are part of this place where God has put us."* But Corrie was convinced that Betsie must be wrong.

Corrie and Betsie began leading worship "services" a couple times each day with some scripture reading and singing. It was amazing to see the atmosphere change as those in their barracks experienced these glimmers of hope. At first, these services were very low-key and secretive in order to keep the guards from finding out. But as time went by, they grew bolder with no guards coming near.

This was a mystery since every other location around the facility had rigid surveillance. No one understood why...until one evening when Corrie and Betsie were waiting in the dinner line. Corrie describes the scene in her book *The Hiding Place*...

*Betsie's eyes were twinkling.*

*You know, we've never understood why we had so much freedom in the big room. Well--I've found out.*

*That afternoon,* she said, *there'd been confusion in her knitting group about sock sizes and they'd asked the supervisor to come and settle it.*

*But she wouldn't. She wouldn't step through the door and neither would the guards. And you know why?*

*Because of the fleas!*

*That's what she said, "That place is crawling with fleas!"*

*My mind rushed back to our first hour in this place. I remembered Betsie's bowed head, remembered her thanks to God for creatures I could see no use for.*

And so, there was reason to be grateful for the little pests after all. In the most miserable of circumstances, God's Word had been put into practice. This powerful example of gratitude has encouraged people around the world to find reason to give thanks in their own situation.

Shortly before Betsie died, she told Corrie, *"There is no pit so deep that God's love is not deeper still."*

May we all live with a spirit of gratitude as we recall Betsie's words.

# Day #11:

"*Feeling gratitude and not expressing it is like wrapping a present and not giving it.*" - William Arthur Ward

*"Make a joyful shout to the Lord, all you lands!*
*Serve the Lord with gladness;*
*Come before His presence with singing.*
*Know that the Lord, He is God;*
*It is He who has made us, and not we ourselves;*
*We are His people and the sheep of His pasture.*
*Enter into His gates with thanksgiving,*
*And into His courts with praise.*
*Be thankful to Him, and bless His name.*
*For the Lord is good;*
*His mercy is everlasting,*
*And His truth endures to all generations."*

~Psalm 100~

## *The Gratitude Challenge:*

One way to express our gratitude to God is through worship music. Play a worship song and sing along or sing a song to the Lord to express your thanks to Him today.

## *Prayer of Gratitude: Healing*

Lord, today I want to thank You for Your healing power in my life. I have experienced Your healing in many ways: spiritually, emotionally and physically. You have come to heal the broken hearted and I thank You for the emotional healing You have brought into my life. There are days that are still difficult, but I know that You are walking with me and that I am not alone. It takes time and patience as You heal me stitch by stitch, but it is worth it.

Thank You for Your healing power that is available to my physical body as well. Jesus, when You walked this earth, one of the ways You demonstrated Your power was to bring physical healing to many...and You continue to do so today. I realize that Your healing may look differently than I expect and I will choose to trust You even when I don't understand all the "why's."

I praise You that I am fearfully and wonderfully made and that You place Your healing hand upon my life each and every day. I love You. Amen.

*"The Spirit of the Lord God is upon Me, because the Lord has anointed Me to preach good tidings to the poor; He has sent Me to heal the brokenhearted, to proclaim liberty to the captives, and the opening of the prison to those who are bound."*

- Isaiah 61:1

*"Yea, though I walk through the valley of the shadow of death, I will fear no evil; for You are with me; Your rod and Your staff, they comfort me."*

- Psalm 23:4

*"And Jesus went about all Galilee, teaching in their synagogues, preaching the gospel of the kingdom, and healing all kinds of sickness and all kinds of disease among the people."*

- Matthew 4:23

*"I will praise You, for I am fearfully and wonderfully made;*
*Marvelous are Your works, And that my soul knows very well."*

- Psalm 139:14

## *Story of Gratitude:*
## *Something To Be Thankful For*
### *Heather Hart*

*"The thief comes only to steal and kill and destroy; I have come that they may have life, and have it to the full."*
- John 10:10 (NIV)

Is it possible to live a life of gratitude when you have a physical abnormality?
Is it possible to give thanks when you will never be able to be like other people?

What if you know, without a shadow of a doubt, that you are scarred for life?

The answer is a resounding "YES!" if you ask Nick Vujicic who was born without any arms or legs.

It was in Brisbane, Australia and the year was 1982, a mother went through a seemingly normal pregnancy and gave birth to her precious baby boy - however, with no medical reasoning, that precious baby boy had no legs, and no arms. Raised in a Christian home, Nick never once wished he had arms and legs, because he knew that wishing wouldn't help. In fact, he says that he thanks God for making him the way He did so that he can reach others for Jesus. That wasn't always the case though; he says that he often struggled with the why. Why was he created limbless? He finally found peace at 15 years old when he truly comprehended that he had someone who not only understood his circumstances, but was also bigger than them. He knew his parents loved him, but they couldn't change anything - God on the other hand, changed his heart.

By the time Nick turned 19 he was already sharing his testimony of victory - not the victory of learning to walk, swim, or play soccer (all of which he can do), but the victory of knowing that God is the one who created him and helps him take each step. The victory of knowing that he is loved so much that God sent His Son, Jesus Christ, to die on the cross for his sins. The victory of living a life of gratitude.

Today, Nick is known world-wide for his incredible passion for life that is lived out loud with an overwhelming amount of gratitude for God. But one thing is clear in all of Nick's talks: It's impossible to be thankful when you're looking at all of the things you can't do. He might not have arms and legs, but he is thankful that he has life - and a full life at that. In one of his talks he brought up how easy it is to focus on the things you don't have, or even the things you wish you didn't have, yet that's not what God wants for us. He doesn't want us to live a life of regrets and resignations, but to live life to its fullest, and to be able to say with Paul, *"I know what it is to be in need, and I know what it is to have plenty. I have learned the secret of being content in any and every situation, whether well fed or hungry, whether living in plenty or in want. I can do everything through him who gives me strength."* Philippians 4:12-13 (NIV)

As Nick always says, *"If God can use a man without arms and legs to be His hands and feet, then He will certainly use any willing heart!"* We can do anything through Christ, no matter what our circumstances. Now that's something to be thankful for.

# Day #12:

"*Today, when stress mounts, I pray to dismount it with gratitude. I can only feel one feeling at a time, and I choose to give thanks at all times. Fight feeling with feeling!*" - Ann Voskamp

"*Be anxious for nothing, but in everything by prayer and supplication, with thanksgiving, let your requests be made known to God; and the peace of God, which surpasses all understanding, will guard your hearts and minds through Christ Jesus.*"

- Philippians 4:6-7

## *The Gratitude Challenge:*

What are you anxious about today? Choose to pray about the situation instead of worry and complain. Find one thing that you can be thankful for about the situation and pray a pray of thanksgiving as well. Even if your heart isn't in it at first, take the step of faith and see what God does.

## Prayer of Gratitude:
## The Body of Christ

Lord, today I want to thank You for the body of Christ, other believers You have placed in my life. Just as my physical body is designed to work together with all of its parts functioning properly, Your Church, the body of Christ is intended to work together as well.

Thank You for the people You strategically place in my life to encourage me when I need it the most. This encouragement may come in the form of encouraging words, a prayer or even a simple smile. Many times I can feel Your love through other believers.

I realize that apart from Jesus, no human being is perfect this side of heaven. Therefore, there will be issues that arise sometimes within the Church. I ask Your forgiveness for the times that I have given into a spirit of gossip, judgment or division. Please forgive me. You long for there to be a spirit of unity and love amongst the body of Christ. I pray that Your love would flow through me to other believers within the Church and that You would show me how to be an encouragement and support to them. Use me as Your light wherever I go. Amen.

*"Just as a body, though one, has many parts, but all its many parts form one body, so it is with Christ."*
                                        - I Corinthians 12:12 (NIV)
*"Two are better than one, because they have a good reward for their labor. For if they fall, one will lift up his companion. But woe to him who is alone when he falls, for*

*he has no one to help him up. Again, if two lie down together, they will keep warm;*
*But how can one be warm alone? Though one may be overpowered by another, two can withstand him. And a threefold cord is not quickly broken."*

- Ecclesiastes 4:9-12

*"Beloved, let us love one another, for love is of God; and everyone who loves is born of God and knows God."*

- I John 4:7

*"I do not pray for these alone, but also for those who will believe in Me through their word; that they all may be one, as You, Father, are in Me, and I in You; that they also may be one in Us, that the world may believe that You sent Me.*

- John 17:20-21

## Story of Gratitude:
## Cameron's Story

### Shelley Hitz

I met Cameron, a vibrant 19 year-old, at a speaking engagement in March 2012. He shared his testimony before we spoke at a youth event one night from his wheelchair because he is paralyzed from the neck down...he is a quadriplegic.

You see, Cameron was in a diving accident at the age of 18.

And the first thing he said after he was rescued from the water was not, *"Why God?!"* But instead, in faith, he said, *"God, by Your stripes I am healed."* His focus was not on his circumstances, but on His God that he knew had the power to heal him. Now remember, this is the response of an 18 year-old teenage boy.

I talked to his mom and she said Cameron's doctor wanted to tell him that he would never use a manual wheelchair...that he would have to use an electric wheelchair for the rest of his life because of the location of his spinal cord damage. And she said, *"Please don't tell my son that. He doesn't believe that. He believes that his God is going to heal him."* The doctor honored her wishes and never mentioned that detail to Cameron. However, when I met Cameron, one year after his accident, he was using a manual wheelchair. He credits God for bringing this healing into his life.

But what is truly amazing about Cameron's story is how he came to this place of amazing faith and gratitude for all Christ has done for him. He said that when he was 16 years-old, he met a family that was different from any family he had ever met before. There was something about this family he desperately wanted - it was Christ in them that made the difference. He began spending time with them and as he did, he started to gain a hunger for the Word of God. Up to that point he had been drinking and smoking and doing what he calls "teenage things." However, he said that all of a sudden, instead of being addicted to "teenage things" he became addicted to the Word of God.

And so, at the age of 16 years-old, he started reading the Bible four hours a day. He said that God was revealing things to him and was pouring into him during that time. Cameron said, *"God knew. He was preparing me."* He said,

*"My foundation was so strong. Because of all the time I had spent in His Word, I knew who my Father was."* And during this time, his spiritual foundation became strong and deep. Therefore, when his crisis hit, instead of viewing God through the crisis, he viewed the crisis through God.

When I heard Cameron's story, I prayed, *"God, I want to be that way. Help me to have a strong foundation in You. Help me to make whatever sacrifices I need to in order to get into Your Word and to spend time with You. Then, when my next crisis comes, I will be ready."* Cameron was ready and God is using him. He is only 19 years-old and yet God is using him in powerful ways as he shares his testimony and how God is continuing to work healing in his life.

How about you? Are you ready? If not, I encourage you to take Cameron's lead and spend more time getting to know your Father through His Word. Make time for God and He will transform you from the inside out.

# Day #13:

I'm only on day 13 and yet I'm finding it harder and harder to think of someone new to send a hand-written thank you card to each day. However, as I took some time to reflect on all I've been given today, I was able to think of another person that blessed us and so another card was written, addressed, stamped and sent out in the mail today.

I have heard that writing something out in a journal (or writing cards like I am each day) does something deeper within us than just saying the words or typing them out. I don't know the exact reason, but I do know that you involve more senses as you write: your sense of touch and sight. And I do think there is value in writing things out. For example, as I write out three things I'm thankful for each day in my journal and as I write out a hand written thank you card, it deepens my focus on the things I am thankful for today and also leaves a record that I can look back upon when I need the encouragement.

*"Hear, O Israel: The Lord our God, the Lord is one! You shall love the Lord your God with all your heart, with all your soul, and with all your strength. And these words which I command you today shall be in your heart. You shall teach them diligently to your children, and shall talk of them when you sit in your house, when you walk by the*

*way, when you lie down, and when you rise up. You shall
bind them as a sign on your hand, and they shall be as
frontlets between your eyes. **You shall write them** on the
doorposts of your house and on your gates."*

- Deuteronomy 6: 4-9

*"Gratitude to God makes even a temporal blessing a taste
of heaven."*

- Wm. Romaine

## The Gratitude Challenge:

Write out what you are thankful for today on a piece of
paper or in your journal. I encourage you to write it out as
a prayer to God. i.e. "Thank you Lord for _____ today
because _____."

## Prayer of Gratitude:
## Faithfulness

Lord, today I want to thank You for Your faithfulness.
Even when I am unfaithful to You, You are always faithful
to me. Great is Your faithfulness.

Amidst a world of changes, You are a God who never
changes. You are the same yesterday, today and forever.
Even when others' opinions of me change, when the
economy changes, when the fashion trends change; You
never change. Thank You for being the solid rock in my
life that I can always depend on.

I thank You, Lord, that You are faithful in ALL You do. I admit that sometimes I don't understand Your ways. But I know that just as a Polaroid picture is fuzzy at first and then later fully develops and is seen clearly, I too will someday see things clearly. You will either reveal it to me later in this life or I will fully understand once I reach heaven. Help me to put my trust in Your faithfulness in the midst of the "fuzziness" of my life.

I am so grateful that You are faithful to forgive my sins when I confess them to You. Your faithfulness touches my life in so many ways. Great is Your faithfulness! Amen.

*"Through the Lord's mercies we are not consumed, because His compassions fail not. They are new every morning; great is Your faithfulness."*
- Lamentations 3:22-23

*"Jesus Christ is the same yesterday, today, and forever."*
- Hebrews 13:8

*"For the word of the Lord is right and true; He is faithful in all He does."*
-Psalm 33:4 (NIV)

*"If we confess our sins, He is faithful and just to forgive us our sins and to cleanse us from all unrighteousness."*
- I John 1:9

## *Story of Gratitude:*
## *God's Story*

*Troy Lewis*

I can remember it like it was yesterday...

Stephanie and I were waiting with eager anticipation, in what was an all too familiar place.

My hospital room.

It felt like forever since I had been home. Even when I was, all I had done was sleep. My mind was always in a fog from my body poisoning itself. But now things were going to be much different. I was heading home with the ultimate mulligan, a do over. Another chance at life!

As we waited, I gazed at Stephanie, thinking about all that we'd been through. She was not only my wife, but my best friend, love of my life, and my caregiver. A task, I would not wish on anyone, but one that I'm forever grateful for.

*        *        *

Just six months earlier, life as I knew it was over. All of the things that I had loved doing (coaching girls fast pitch softball and playing Jesus in our local passion play) suddenly came to an end. I had reached kidney failure at the young age of 42.

I would question God over and over again. Asking, "Why? Why would You allow this to happen?"

I would go on dialysis, only to find out it didn't work for me. It was hurting me more than helping. The one thing that was supposed to keep me alive, was hastening my death.

Just a couple months later, I was sitting on my bed, waiting on a phone call when the phone rang.

It was my brother.

He was the last of my four brothers to tell me that he too was not a match. Four brothers, four opportunities at a second chance at life, and none could be used.

I stood there thinking about the hopelessness of it all.

I hung the phone up and dropped it down to my side in defeat only to turn and see my wife standing there with a look of sheer shock on her face. We began to cry our eyes out all night long, wondering where God was in all this. Why He would create such a hopeless situation?

\*     \*     \*

Then just five days later, I was laying in intensive care wondering how much longer I would last and how many days I had left. I wondered why God would take me this way, leaving behind a wife and two daughters.

With my body shutting down, I surrendered to God, accepting defeat to death. I knew my time was finished unless a miracle happened. *"Lord If you take me I'm yours.*

*And if you leave me here I'm yours. So whether you take me or leave me, I'm yours Lord"*

Those were the words I prayed to God as I laid there.

48 hours later on July 28th, God would begin raining down his grace and mercy, stretching out His hands to give me my life back in the most amazing way.

All those months that I was suffering, praying, holding on to faith, and wondering where God was going with this, He had been convicting a stranger from 1,000 miles away to give his kidney away, for no other reason than "God led him to." No other reason. This man had no idea that he had the rarest of kidneys and that he was not only going to save my life, but my brother's life too.

Two days after my surgery, my brother would give his kidney for my payment. He had complications that would nearly cost him his life. However, we found out afterwards that if he hadn't been the one chosen, he wouldn't have made it through the year.

God is so awesome! Not only did he save me by his grace on Easter Sunday of 2000, He now saved me by His mercy in 2010, along with my brother.

I remember leaving the hospital that day. The sun was making its way down to dusk. I had a feeling of complete peace, freedom, and tranquility. It felt like I'd been cleansed and given a new beginning.

I just gazed out the window at the sun setting, with a smile on my face that would not leave. Tears began to well up...until they overflowed. My heart was humbly overflowing with love and appreciation of everyone that had ever prayed and believed, and even those that prayed and doubted.

They were not alone, there were many times I doubted too.

I stared into the sunset as if it were God's eyes. In the deepest appreciation of my Savior's gift, I knew I was spared for a reason. It was too dramatic. Almost like a modern day Bible story. Actually some have called it just that.

This was a God directed true story that I have vowed to share with the whole world. It is not mine, it is God's. He has allowed me to live so that I can share it.

In our local passion drama ministry I played the role of Jesus for 9 years - the same drama that led me to Christ on Easter Sunday of 2000. I shared my testimony after each performance to bring others to Christ.

All this to prepare for the next step.

God has set me on a new course now. One I was not comfortable with, but I knew I had to do.

God put it on my heart to write His story down and tell it to everyone. The book is titled, "Another Second Chance." And my testimony that I share at churches, groups, and organizations is called "God's Story."

*"I consider that our present sufferings are not worth comparing with the glory that will be revealed in us."*
- Romans 8:18 (NIV)

*"And we know that in all things God works for the good of those who love him, who have been called according to his purpose."*
- Romans 8:28 (NIV)

*"What, then, shall we say in response to these things? If God is for us, who can be against us?"*
- Romans 8:31 (NIV)

# Day #14:

*"A thankful heart enjoys blessings twice – when they're received, and when they're remembered."* - Selected

*"And give thanks for everything to God the Father in the name of our Lord Jesus Christ."*

- Ephesians 5:20

## The Gratitude Challenge:

Learn to enjoy your blessings twice.  :)

## Prayer of Gratitude:
## The Bible

Lord, today I am thankful for Your Word, the Bible, which You use to speak to me.   Your Word is a lamp unto my feet and a light unto my path.   When I feel confused and not sure what to do, I can look to Your Word which will guide me and lead me.

I am thankful that You chose to inspire men to write down Your words.   You are the author; they were merely the vessels You used. I praise You that the Bible has been so well preserved through the years so that it could be passed down to us today.

Lord, help me to never take the Bible for granted. Give me a renewed passion and thirst for Your Word and to know You better through it. As I read it, memorize it and study it; I am getting to know You in a deeper way - the creator of this universe. Thank You that You choose to make Yourself known to me in many ways including the Bible.

And as the grass withers and the flowers fade away, I praise You that Your Word stands FOREVER!! Amen.

*"Your word is a lamp to my feet and a light to my path."*
- Psalm 119:105

*"For prophecy never came by the will of man, but holy men of God spoke as they were moved by the Holy Spirit."*
- 2 Peter 1:21

*"All Scripture is given by inspiration of God, and is profitable for doctrine, for reproof, for correction, for instruction in righteousness."*
- 2 Timothy 3:16

*"The grass withers, the flower fades, but the word of our God stands forever."*
- Isaiah 40:8

# Story of Gratitude:
## A Breath of Fresh Air

*CJ Hitz*

*"Let everything that breathes sing praises to the Lord!
Praise the Lord!"*

- Psalm 150:6 (NLT)

At times, we're all guilty of taking certain things in life for granted. For some, it might be the fact that they have a good paying job. For others, it might be the beautiful home where they reside. Many of us take our family members for granted...until we lose one of them.

Recently, I've found myself grateful for something more than any other time in my life. That 'something' is...*Air*. More specifically, the ability to breathe that air the way my Creator intended.

If you've ever lived near a forest fire, you know a little of what I'm talking about. When we moved to Colorado Springs, little did we know that within two months, we'd find ourselves near the worst forest fire in Colorado history. About 350 homes were destroyed along with over 18,000 acres of forest charred to a crisp. Think of Mordor in *Lord of the Rings*.

Shelley noticed a plume of smoke coming over the ridge that we can see out our front window. It was coming from the Waldo Canyon area, a popular spot for both runners and hikers alike. A couple hours later, I decided to head out for a 12 mile run despite the smoke continuing to saturate the 90 degree dry air. This was Saturday June 23, 2012.

The next day, Shelley and I closed our windows and hunkered inside to monitor the fire online via news reports and a myriad of Twitter activity. The fire was growing. I decided this was a good day to rest from running, especially after the effort I exerted on that 12 mile run a day earlier. But like many runners after a day off, come Monday I was getting antsy. By this time, the fire had continued to grow and the smoke had saturated the air even further.

Against my better judgment, I proceeded to head out the door for an easy 6 mile run, totally underestimating the effect it might have on my lungs. Almost immediately I found myself laboring more than usual in my breathing. At first, I thought it might be some fatigue from Saturday's run. "Surely I'll push through it after a mile or two", I thought to myself. Unfortunately, relief never came. I literally felt like I had taken three steps back in my training and fitness overnight! After finishing this tortured run, I looked down at my watch and noticed a slow-as-molasses pace.

It was the next day, Tuesday June 26$^{th}$ that will be forever remembered as one of the worst in Colorado Springs history. What had already become an out-of-control fire, turned into a raging inferno devouring everything in its path. In a span of a few hours, it grew from 5,000 to 15,000 acres in size thanks to sinister 80mph winds (hurricane strength!) howling in every direction. Firefighters had never seen so many horrific conditions come together at once. It seemed as if the fire had a personality of its own.

Putting yesterday's slogging run behind me, I decided to head down to Carmichael Training Systems where they were allowing local athletes to get some relief from smoke and heat by using their equipment free of charge. I decided to do a speed workout that would include twelve repeats of 400 meters each with a short rest between each rep. Keep in mind that I'd done this workout with no problem the week before. As I started the treadmill and began my warm-up, I could feel my breathing was still labored. "*This is weird*," I thought to myself. After completing my warm-up, I increased the speed for my first repeat and struggled to hold the pace. After three of these I decided it was time to bag the workout and turn the speed down to very easy pace. By the time I finished, I was shaking my head in disbelief at how difficult the easy pace felt.

Something was wrong and I was frustrated.

Part of my frustration was the fact that I was a mere 7 ½ weeks from the Pikes Peak Ascent. This is a race I'd had on my calendar for months now. My training had been going well up to that point, my body adjusting more and more to the Colorado altitude. Now I had no other choice but to take some days off and 'test the waters' to see if I was improving. Another two weeks went by and I was no better. I'd been scouring the internet in hopes of diagnosing my problem. Could it be anemia? Collapsed lung? Exercised-induced asthma? I was going down one rabbit trail after another and getting nowhere fast.

It was now time to do the unthinkable…seek out a local doctor. I couldn't recall the last time I needed to see a doctor. I had a prideful attitude regarding my health. I think I began to put more faith in my machine-like body than the God who knit that body together. Between eating a healthy diet and running 50 miles a week, what could possibly go wrong with this fine body of mine? How arrogant to think I was above being vulnerable to any ailment as if I'd tapped into the fountain of youth.

A running friend of mine recommended a local doctor who'd served as a physician on the last couple Olympic teams. I called his office and was able to go in the next day for some tests. A chest x-ray revealed no collapsed lung which was a relief. A breathing test showed that I was a little less than average for my age. Finally, they took some blood samples to determine whether I had anemia or some other disease. The doctor called a couple days later to inform me that my blood work was fine with no deficiencies whatsoever. Another relief.

With no history of asthma, the most-likely cause of my labored breathing while running was smoke getting into my lungs. The doctor recommended I try an inhaler for two weeks and slowly work into some running. Even the thought of puffing on an inhaler stung my pride but I was desperate and willing to try anything. After forking over a whopping $125 (ouch!) for this little breathing aid, I commenced with two puffs a day during the first few days before weaning down to one puff each day.

I was also being lifted up in prayer by my wonderful wife and other family members who had been concerned. After taking several days completely off, I began to run again. Miraculously, I felt stronger with each new run! My breathing wasn't labored like it had been. I could pick up the pace without shortness of breath occurring so quickly. Running up hills didn't feel as painful.

I COULD RUN...AND BREATHE!!!!

As my lungs were being filled with more air, I could feel my heart being filled with more gratitude. Each breath is a gift from God Almighty. Job knew this well, even in the midst of trial...

*"For the life of every living thing is in his hand, and the breath of every human being."*

- Job 12:10 (NLT)

Thankfully, the worst forest fire in Colorado history is behind us now. The smoke is gone and we have access to clean air again. I've learned a few lessons along the way. I have a greater appreciation for firefighters and I cherish rain like never before.

Thank you Lord for the gifts you lavish on us each day. Gifts like air and running.

# Day #15:

*"Ingratitude is always a form of weakness. I have never known a man of real ability to be ungrateful."* - Goethe

Even Jesus displayed a spiritual of gratefulness to His Father.

*"So they rolled the stone aside. Then Jesus looked up to heaven and said, 'Father, thank you for hearing me. You always hear me, but I said it out loud for the sake of all these people standing here, so that they will believe you sent me.'"*

- John 11:41-42

*"So they rolled the stone aside. Then Jesus looked up to heaven and said, "Father, thank you for hearing me."*

- John 11:41

## *The Gratitude Challenge:*

Think of the people of "real ability" in your life. Do they display an attitude of gratefulness or a complaining spirit? Which do you want to be known for in your life? Let's follow the example of Jesus and display thankfulness in our lives.

## Prayer of Gratitude:
## *Faith*

Lord, thank You that You are not only the author of my faith but also the perfecter of my faith. I ask that You continue to perfect my faith as many times I still waver in unbelief. I confess my unbelief to You right now. As the father said to Jesus about healing his son, "I do believe; help me overcome my unbelief." I ask Your forgiveness and pray for the strength to believe in You despite my circumstances.

I also realize that without faith it is impossible to please You. Impossible. Help me to remember this when doubts slip into my mind and lies from the enemy tempt me to not believe Your promises. Strengthen me with power from Your Holy Spirit to have faith that stands the test of time.

Thank You for equipping me with the shield of faith to fight the battles that wage in my mind. With my shield of faith raised high, I can quench the fiery darts from the enemy that seek to destroy me.

And right now I affirm my faith and belief in You, Lord. I believe, I believe, I do believe! Amen.

*"Let us fix our eyes on Jesus, the author and perfecter of our faith, who for the joy set before him endured the cross, scorning its shame, and sat down at the right hand of the throne of God."*
- Hebrews 12:2 (NIV)

*"Immediately the boy's father exclaimed, 'I do believe; help me overcome my unbelief!'"*

- Mark 9:24 (NIV)

*"But without faith it is impossible to please Him, for he who comes to God must believe that He is, and that He is a rewarder of those who diligently seek Him."*

- Hebrews 11:6

*"Above all, taking the shield of faith with which you will be able to quench all the fiery darts of the wicked one."*

- Ephesians 6:16

## *Story of Gratitude: A Merry Heart Does Good...*

### *Phyllis Sather*

*"A merry heart does good, like medicine, But a broken spirit dries the bones."*

- Proverbs 17:22

Born seven weeks early, our son Eric has been an ongoing source of inspiration to me. Instead of a two month hospital stay, he left in six days. He was small, just five pounds, but a real fighter.

Nurses told us preemies don't nurse - especially boys. Nursing our daughters had been such a positive experience that I really wanted to nurse Eric, too. My husband Dan, a physician, knew Eric couldn't afford to lose any weight so he thought I should bottle-feed him as suggested. After three months on bed rest and an emergency C-section I

101

wasn't going too far, so I begged Dan to let me just take Eric to bed with me and let him nurse whenever he would. I agreed to bottle him if he lost any weight. He ended up gaining almost a pound the first week and nursed for two years, which turned out to be a real blessing and leads me to my next point.

When he was 16 months old he got an ear infection. After two series of antibiotics he woke up Sunday morning crying and couldn't be consoled. His temperature was 103 degrees, so our pediatrician said we should take him to Children's Hospital. They ran a series of tests, decided to admit him, and then told us they thought he had leukemia. We were stunned! How do you go from an ear infection to leukemia? By Tuesday the diagnosis had been confirmed and he had his first bone marrow biopsy, a Hickman catheter put into his chest, and by Wednesday he had the first in a long series of blood transfusions.

The day before Eric's hospitalization a song based on this verse kept running through my husband's mind:

*"Being confident of this very thing that he which hath begun a good work in you will perform until the day of Jesus Christ.""* Philippians 1:6 (KJV)

During these first days we chose it as Eric's life verse. We didn't think it was a guarantee that he would live, but it helped us believe that the Lord would fulfill the purposes He had for Eric - and us.

My big question was why this had to happen to Eric when he was so young. He was the last male child in my husband's family. We had waited and prayed for him for years, and now this.

We entered the world of cancer. Eric would have to undergo three and a half years of chemotherapy. Just the sight of blood made me sick, and now I would have to live in the hospital world for over three years. When the nurse came to teach me how to change the dressing on his catheter, I quickly replied, *"Oh, my husband will do that."* Her reply was, *"Mrs. Sather, we can let you take your son home as soon as you learn to change the dressing."* Needless to say, I drew on God's grace and learned how to change the dressing. It was a task I would do every other day for the next three years.

With leukemia you never know what a day will bring. Eric would wake up from a nap with a temperature, or he would have a reaction to one of the chemotherapy drugs, or his catheter would fall out, all of which meant emergency hospital visits or even surgery. By the time he was two years old he had undergone more surgeries than most people have in a lifetime. He had bone marrow biopsies every third month. I would hold him while they pumped the anesthesia into his catheter. One minute he would be talking and playing and the next he would go as limp as death in my arms, after which I would hand him to a nurse and race out of the room, sobbing.

Angry with God, I would ask why my baby had to go through all of this.

Eric responded quite differently, entering every day with a big smile on his face and a baggie of Cheerios in his hand.

103

The nurses said they could always tell when Eric was around because there were Cheerios everywhere. His little two-year-old hands would drop as many as he ate. He knew all the routines. If the nurses missed a step in preparing him for a test or for surgery he would stop them and remind them of what they were supposed to do next. He knew everyone and had a smile for them all.

One day we were in for a bone marrow biopsy. As we were going through the regular routine of preparation there was a boy next to us who was about three years old and had just been diagnosed with leukemia. There was a big difference in how he was handling all the procedures. He was fighting and crying and refusing to let the nurses do what needed to be done. It was then the Lord spoke to my heart. Eric had been so young when he was diagnosed that these procedures were a way of life for him. He didn't know anything else and didn't think to question them. When he learned his body parts he would proudly announce his Hickman as one of them.

It was then I yielded my heart to the Lord's wisdom in this situation and saw my biggest question answered. Yes, Eric had been very young to be diagnosed with such a difficult disease, but the Lord had used that for good in his life. I could finally be grateful for the Lord's timing - even in this.

Eric is 21 years old now. He still enters every day with a big smile, but he has gotten rid of the Cheerios. He is healthy and well-rounded, enjoys talking about almost everything, loves all sports, but also enjoys shopping, especially in little gift shops. I keep saying he will make someone a great husband someday.

# Day #16:

I had tears in my eyes after watching this video, "The Amazing Story of Ian and Larissa," that my friend, Renee, recommended to me: http://www.godtube.com/watch/?v= WLDGDGNX. In the video they show how they created a "Gratitude Board" to remind them of what they are thankful for each day. And so, I felt prompted to also create a Gratitude Board in our house...and luckily my husband agreed. :)

*"Cultivate a thankful spirit! It will be to thee a perpetual feast. There is, or ought to be, with us no such thing as small mercies; all are great, because the least are undeserved. Indeed a really thankful heart will extract motive for gratitude from everything, making the most even of scanty blessings."* - J.R. MacDuff

*"Therefore I exhort first of all that supplications, prayers, intercessions, and giving of thanks be made for all men."*
- I Timothy 2:1

## *The Gratitude Challenge:*

Consider starting a "Gratitude Board" of your own. It could simply be anything you want it to be. For example, you can write something on your mirror with a dry erase marker that you are thankful for that day.

Use your imagination, but here are a few other examples of what you can use to create your gratitude board:

- Mirror
- Chalkboard
- Dry erase board
- Poster board
- Cork board
- Or simply use sticky notes

It is a tangible way to keep your focus on all that you have to be grateful for each day.

If you want to use the heading and quotes I used on our board, you can download them and print them off here: http://gratitude.s3.amazonaws.com/gratitude-board.pdf

## *Prayer of Gratitude: Laughter and Joy*

Lord, today I want to thank You for laughter. A deep belly laugh truly is medicine for the soul. Laughter is an expression of joy and I long to experience Your joy in my life each day. I realize that joy is different than happiness. Happiness is dependent on happenings and my circumstances whereas I find joy in You.

I ask that You help me to have child-like faith so that I can find joy in each day. There is nothing better than seeing a child's face light up with a smile and laugh at the smallest things in life. They find joy in everyday life. Help me to be filled with Your Holy Spirit and Your joy, as one of the fruit of Your Spirit is joy. I thank You that in Your Presence is fullness of joy!

However, I admit that sometimes my feelings are up and down. Some days I don't feel like laughing and that's okay too. There is a season for everything: a time to laugh and a time to cry; a time to grieve and a time to dance. Even when I am walking through dark and difficult times, You are with me and You comfort me. Thank You Lord that even in the difficult days, Your joy can be my strength. Amen.

*"A cheerful heart is good medicine, but a crushed spirit dries up the bones."*

- Proverbs 17:22 (NIV)

*"But the fruit of the Spirit is love, joy, peace, longsuffering, kindness, goodness, faithfulness, gentleness, self-control. Against such there is no law."*

- Galatians 5:22-23

*"You will show me the path of life; in Your presence is fullness of joy; at Your right hand are pleasures forevermore."*

- Psalms 16:11

*"To everything there is a season, a time for every purpose under heaven...a time to weep, and a time to laugh; a time to mourn, and a time to dance."*

- Ecclesiastes 3:1, 4

*"Yea, though I walk through the valley of the shadow of death, I will fear no evil; for You are with me; Your rod and Your staff, they comfort me."*

- Psalm 23:4

*"Do not sorrow, for the joy of the Lord is Your strength."*

- Nehemiah 8:10b

## Story of Gratitude:
## Gratitude For Bodily Functions

*Sheri Ketner*

During my husband, Keith's, 23 day stay in the CCU at Ross Heart Hospital there were many extreme ups and downs. God was near to us the entire time but during certain special times we knew He was breathing on our shoulders and even on our lungs.

One particular day, we were all waiting for Keith's organs to come back around from the hit they had taken from multiple surgeries for a heart bypass. His kidneys had not been operating very well. One nurse described it as *"when your heart has taken the hits his has, then the organs are delayed from the hit as well."* Medication was given to him during a five day period to put him in an induced coma to allow his organs to "rest".

During morning rounds one particular day, I heard the nurse tell one of the doctors that Keith's output was better. The doctor seemed more pleased and almost giddy at the news. After the tribe of five or six doctors went to the next room I asked the nurse *"So what's the big deal?"* She then explained that because he had so many drugs in his system, it was a major concern that the kidneys were not functioning. *"So this is a blessing huh?"* *"Yes, it is a very good sign,"* she said. *"Sometimes the patient needs to go on dialysis for a while if their kidneys don't start back up,"* she replied.

The next day he had a bowel movement that needed to be cleaned up. Mind you, when he did open his eyes during the four to five days of his induced coma, you could tell no one was home. I don't think he even knows to this day that he made this mess. However, it was the first news the night nurse gave to the day nurse, and there was obvious joy between the two.

## My Lesson in Gratitude:

Blessings come in unique ways. Whether it is money coming in the mail you weren't expecting, finding an old friend on Facebook, or a verse you were looking for to apply to your situation. Blessings can also come in bodily functions when your loved one's body is trying to shut down from being critically ill.

Thank you, Lord, for showing up one more time on behalf of Keith this day.

# Day #17:

Wow...it is hard to believe that today is already day 17 for me in the gratitude challenge. Only 4 more days left, but already God has been blessing me through taking the time to focus on Him and all that He has given me. Instead of being down and feeling self-pity about being in a new place without a church home or friends, I have been focused on all that He has given me. And in the process I am watching as He is providing relationships for me as well as community with other believers. How amazing is that? Thank you Lord for providing what I need as I trust you and keep my focus on all that you've given me.

*"If you have a special need today, focus your full attention on the goodness and greatness of your Father rather than on the size of your need. Your need is tiny compared to His ability to meet it."* - Bill Patterson

*"If you, then, though you are evil, know how to give good gifts to your children, how much more will your Father in heaven give good gifts to those who ask him!"*
- Matthew 7:11 (NIV)

*"And my God will meet all your needs according to his glorious riches in Christ Jesus."*
- Philippians 4:19 (NIV)

## *The Gratitude Challenge:*

Instead of focusing on the biggest need in your life today, focus on Christ and what He has given you. Every time that big need comes to mind and threatens to take over, surrender it again to Jesus thanking Him for providing the answer even before you can see your prayer answered. Trust that He will provide everything you need.

## *Prayer of Gratitude:*
## *Spiritual Gifts*

Lord, today I want to thank You for the spiritual gifts You have given me. There are many different spiritual gifts, but they all come from You. Thank You that You give gifts to every one of us within the body of Christ, including myself. No one has been left empty handed. Even if the gifts You have given me do not seem as important as another person's, they are essential to the body of Christ, the Church. Just as my intestines are as important as my eyes in my physical body, You created the Church to work together with the gifts You have given us in unity.

I pray that You would continue to reveal to me what my spiritual gifts are...some are apostles, prophets, evangelists, pastors and teachers. And yet You've also given us gifts of prophesy, serving, encouragement, giving and leading. And these are just a few of the gifts You have given us. Next, empower me to use the gifts You've given to me. Help me to be obedient to use my gifts no matter how insignificant they may seem.

111

I also thank You when someone uses their gifts to bless me. Thank You for those that have taught me Your Word, given generously to me, served me and encouraged me. Thank You for using others in powerful ways in my life. Amen.

*"There are diversities of gifts, but the same Spirit. There are differences of ministries, but the same Lord. And there are diversities of activities, but it is the same God who works all in all."*
- I Corinthians 12: 4-6

*"But in fact God has placed the parts in the body, every one of them, just as he wanted them to be. If they were all one part, where would the body be? As it is, there are many parts, but one body."*
- I Corinthians 12:18-20 (NIV)

*"And He Himself gave some to be apostles, some prophets, some evangelists, and some pastors and teachers, for the equipping of the saints for the work of ministry, for the edifying of the body of Christ"*
- Ephesians 4:11-12

*"We have different gifts, according to the grace given to each of us. If your gift is prophesying, then prophesy in accordance with your faith; if it is serving, then serve; if it is teaching, then teach; if it is to encourage, then give encouragement; if it is giving, then give generously; if it is to lead, do it diligently; if it is to show mercy, do it cheerfully."*
- Romans 12:6-8 (NIV)

## *Story of Gratitude:*
## *Keeping Me Going*

*Kimberly Rae*

A tiny part of my body does not function correctly. Because of this, I live my life on a strict schedule of pills, pills and more pills, not to mention a special diet, restricted activity, etc. You get the picture.

I am 37 years old. Too young many would say to be doing all this extra stuff just to keep going. Sometimes I think that same thought to myself, along with other thoughts like:

*"It's not fair."*
*"Why me?"*
*"I could do so much more for God if I was healthy."*

My health brought us home from the mission field. My health has limited our involvement in church, and even our ability to have people in our home. I have wanted to feel sorry for myself. I have wanted to explain to people that I really would do more if I could. To make sure everyone knows it's not my fault that taking care of my body is my full-time job.

This morning after a handful of pills, my yucky-tasting liquid medication, and my specialized breakfast, I was thinking of how much effort it takes just to replace (or try to replace) the function of one, extremely small part of my body.

Suddenly it was as if the Lord opened my eyes. I was complaining about how much I had to invest in keeping my

113

own body running. But I'm only "helping out" a part that's about the size of my thumbnail. All the rest - the organs, tissues, the millions and millions of cells - God's been keeping all that running every moment of every day my entire life.

"The human body is comprised of billions of microscopic units, each with their own unique function yet all working together to create one smoothly operating entity." (How the Body Works) Each human body has over 200 bones, over 600 muscles, 10 trillion cells, and over 100,000 hairs (well, most of us anyway). Those are impossible numbers for my mind to visualize, much less truly comprehend. I wouldn't be able to even calculate all that is going on in my body at any given moment, much less keep it going.

The heart pumps over 1,500 gallons of blood each day, beating 100,000 times. Each person breathes thousands of times per day, most of those breaths taken without conscious thought.
Imagine if you had to tell yourself to breathe each moment, tell your heart to beat, consciously blink your eyelids, digest your food, see, hear, taste. And that's just things that are happening physically. Don't forget your mind. Can you imagine having to process and store the thousands of thoughts that come to mind each day?

Millions of things are functioning within each of our bodies all day long without any effort on our part.

And here I am complaining because I have to be responsible for about 20 more than the average person, thinking life isn't fair.

May God forgive my lack of understanding and self-centeredness.

People ask sometimes why God allows bad things to happen. Why are some people in wheelchairs? Why do some people's bodies not do what they are supposed to do?

Maybe we are looking at things backwards. Instead of asking why things aren't as good as they "should" be, why don't we ask why things are as good as they are?

Why do our bodies function at all?

Why can we wake up each morning and breathe freely without even trying?

Why do our hearts keep beating without us telling them to?

When my husband was growing up, if he ever complained to his dad that he was bored, his dad would assign him a chore to do. He learned quickly that being bored wasn't the worst thing that could happen to him!

God is keeping my body going every moment of every day. But most of the time, I don't even think about it, until something doesn't work the way it "should," and I start complaining.

Perhaps God has allowed my health problems to remind me how much of me He has taken responsibility to keep going, showing me how much I have to be thankful for, and indeed how little I have to complain about.

Life is a gift, and every part of our bodies that works is a gift. I start to consider how life would be if I had to be responsible for 40 or 50 or 100 of the millions of things happening to keep my body functioning. When I look at it that way, suddenly instead of complaining, I feel thankful that I only have to keep track of 20 or so!

Therefore, this day that the Lord has made, I will try to take my pills and do my routine with a joyful heart, thankful that I'm not in charge of all my organs and cells and a million other things God is doing for me.

God says I am fearfully and wonderfully made. It's time I did more than just say I believe that. It's time I lived like it too.

# Day #18:

I have a friend, Katie Marie Rowden, who says one way God romances her is to show her hearts everywhere...heart shaped rocks, heart shaped dirt clots, etc. She has a Facebook group for women called, "The Romanced..." https://www.facebook.com/groups/301944103214619 where she and others post ways God romances them each day.

I have been walking and jogging along the same path for the last 6 weeks and until two days ago, I didn't notice ANY hearts. Then, all of a sudden I started to see hearts everywhere. Yesterday I decided to take some pictures and there were sooooo many more that I didn't stop to capture. Originally, I had felt like looking for hearts was Katie's thing, but yesterday I sensed God saying it was also His way of showing me that day how much He loves me and is providing for me (which He is!). So, as I was walking along seeing rocks that resembled hearts and feeling loved by my Savior, I prayed and asked God if He would show me a rock that was almost perfectly shaped as a heart...and He did!! I'm feeling very loved today :)

As I'm in the middle of this 21 day gratitude challenge, God was reminding me yesterday that you find what you look for in life. When we were looking at purchasing a

Toyota RV, I suddenly saw them everywhere. After we bought our car, I saw the same make/model everywhere.

So just like seeing these hearts today along my running path that have been there all along, when we look for something to be thankful for in our life, we'll find it. However, when we look for the negative in our lives, we'll find it as well. It's all a matter of what you are looking for.

## *The Gratitude Challenge:*

Is your focus currently on your problems or on Jesus and all that He has given you today? I encourage you to look for something to be thankful for today!

*"The longer I live, the more I realize the impact of attitude on life. Attitude, to me, is more important than facts. It is more important than the past, the education, the money, than circumstances, than failure, than successes, than what other people think or say or do. It is more important than appearance, giftedness or skill. It will make or break a company... a church... a home. The remarkable thing is we have a choice everyday regarding the attitude we will embrace for that day. We cannot change our past... we cannot change the fact that people will act in a certain way. We cannot change the inevitable. The only thing we can do is play on the one string we have, and that is our attitude. I am convinced that life is 10% what happens to me and 90% of how I react to it. And so it is with you... we are in charge of our Attitudes."* - Charles R. Swindoll

*"Therefore we also, since we are surrounded by so great a cloud of witnesses, let us lay aside every weight, and the sin which so easily ensnares us, and let us run with endurance the race that is set before us, __looking unto Jesus__, the author and finisher of our faith, who for the joy that was set before Him endured the cross, despising the shame, and has sat down at the right hand of the throne of God."*

- Hebrews 12:1-2 (NKJV)

## *Prayer of Gratitude: Self Control*

Lord, today I want to thank You for self-control. As Your child, I have access to Your Holy Spirit. And the fruit of the Holy Spirit is self-control. I thank You for providing me with everything I need; however, I confess that sometimes I lack self-control. I ask for Your forgiveness today. Fill me anew with Your Spirit and Your self-control for every situation I will face.

Sometimes it feels like temptation has overtaken me, but You promise to be faithful and always provide a way of escape. Empower me to take Your way of escape when You offer it to me. Thank You Lord that I can have victory over temptation and self-control when I am empowered by Your Spirit. May I walk in that victory today. Amen.

*"But the fruit of the Spirit is love, joy, peace, longsuffering, kindness, goodness, faithfulness, gentleness, self-control. Against such there is no law."*

- Galatians 5:22-23

*"No temptation has overtaken you except such as is common to man; but God is faithful, who will not allow you to be tempted beyond what you are able, but with the temptation will also make the way of escape, that you may be able to bear it."*

- I Corinthians 10:13

*"For God gave us a spirit not of fear but of power and love and self-control."*

- 2 Timothy 1:7 (ESV)

## *Story of Gratitude:*
## *God Reaches Out to Lift Us From Our Troubles*
### *Kathryn Holmes*

*"O afflicted city, lashed by storms, and not comforted, I will rebuild you..."*

- Isaiah 54:11 (NIV)

In 2008 my husband, Charlie, and I were both facing life threatening medical challenges. That year Charlie was in and out of the hospital resulting in quadruple bypass surgery and later a below the knee amputation due to a diabetic infection. My autoimmune disease had returned and I was being treated with large doses of prednisone and chemotherapy. My strength was deteriorating by the day. After three trips to the hospital with fractured vertebrae, on November 1, 2008 I collapsed in my bedroom doorway. Hospital physicians told me I would be paralyzed for the rest of my life.

*"But those who hope in the Lord will renew their strength.
They will soar on wings like eagles; they will run and not
grow weary, they will walk and not be faint."*
- Isaiah 40:31 (NIV)

Since we moved into our condo six years prior to our
medical quagmire, Charlie and I had driven by the neatly
trimmed church on our corner many times. The vibrant
stain glass windows glowing in the sunshine tempted us.
We would say, *"We need to try that church sometime."*
God works in mysterious ways. While Charlie and I were
both recovering in the same rehab center the pastor from
that church came to visit us. A friend of a worried friend
had asked him to see us. We felt very comfortable talking
to him. When I got home and was better able to maneuver
my power chair, I began wheeling up to church. Sunday
after Sunday I kept going with never a rainy day to prevent
me from my trek.

Charlie was more hesitant to commit to a church. Seeing
the peace I found at church he decided to join me. I had my
power chair, but Charlie was in a regular wheelchair and
could not wheel himself that far. We called the mobility
bus to drive us the one block to church. What followed
were two new members. Is there any coincidence in God's
world? I don't think so.

Charlie and I agree that since we have become active in
church - along with volunteering for special projects, I
teach Sunday School and Charlie is in the choir - we have
not had any physical trauma in our lives. Oh, did I leave out
the fact that I am now standing, walking and even driving.

In fact, Charlie packs his walker in the back seat and we actually drive up to church.

Our illnesses took a lot away from us. But, we are so grateful that God rewarded us so handsomely not only with our health, but in our lives.

*"He stilled the storm to a whisper; the waves of the sea were hushed."*
                                                    - Psalm 107:29 (NIV)

The joy and gratitude began to blossom. After thirty-seven years my daughter found just the right man. Although both Charlie and I were both in wheelchairs we fully participated in our daughter's wedding. I was so exhilarated I even danced in my power chair with a girlfriend on my lap. It was such a beautiful wedding I thought I experienced the peak of joy.

*"You will go out in joy and be led forth in peace; the mountains and hills will burst into song before you, and all the trees of the field will clap their hands."*
                                                    - Isaiah 55:12 (NIV)

Then, less than a year later they blessed us with a lovely granddaughter. She was my motivation for becoming more mobile. I wanted to be a "proper" grandmother. I am so thankful that I learned to walk with my first granddaughter and now I chase after my second granddaughter on my own.

After spending much time contemplating his future, my son went back to school, has now completed his schoolwork, and is a licensed pharmacist. His career will blossom and a new life is just beginning for him.

When I was lying in the hospital unable to even roll over in bed, I silently prayed to God not to make me a burden for my husband or my children. Instead he showed me that no matter how bad the storm we can weather it with His help. And when the sun comes out it shines brighter than ever before. We are indeed a blessed, and very grateful, family.

*"May the God of hope fill you with all joy and peace as you trust in Him, so that you may overflow with hope by the power of the Holy Spirit."*

- Romans 15:13 (NIV)

# Day #19:

Yesterday I had one of those days that negative emotions threatened to overtake me. At the same time that I'm taking this gratitude challenge, I'm also working on having better balance in my life and not allowing workaholism to dominate. Well, I have had better balance and am so thankful for that breakthrough. However, yesterday I was thinking about some upcoming project deadlines that I have and began to freak out, wondering how I was going to get it all done. I was on a day trip with my husband when this tsunami of negative emotions threatened to ruin my day. Even in the midst of beautiful scenery on an amazing hike, emotions like...worry, anxiety, fear, a complaining spirit, etc. started to descend upon me.

Then, I began to sense God asking me to change my focus. Instead of complaining about all that I have to do, I started thanking God for the opportunities He has given me. It wasn't an instant change, but it did help and gradually my focus returned again to God and not my deadlines. I then began to pray and ask God for wisdom on how to accomplish all that is on my plate. Throughout the day, I realized that two of my projects had self-imposed deadlines that I could delay if needed. And suddenly I didn't feel so overwhelmed anymore.

I remember a friend of mine saying that she struggled with picking up her husband's dirty socks on their bedroom floor and doing laundry for her family. She found herself grumbling and complaining about it on almost a daily basis. And yet, she sensed God asking her to change her perspective. Instead of complaining about picking up dirty socks, she started thanking God that she has a husband to pick up socks for...a husband that provides for her and loves her. And instead of complaining about doing her kid's laundry, she would thank God that she has children to wash clothes for...children that are healthy and that add so much to her life.

It sounds easy, right?

But, when our emotions start to take over, it no longer feels so easy to be thankful. However, what I found out yesterday is that if you take the step of faith and start thanking God in your situation – even when you don't yet feel thankful – it can change you and your entire day!

## The Gratitude Challenge:

Don't give into the negative emotions that want to take you under today. I encourage you to identify one thing that you often find yourself complaining about in your life. Then, ask God for at least one thing you can be thankful for in that situation and when tempted to complain, allow gratitude to be on your lips instead.

*"It is impossible to feel grateful and depressed in the same moment."* - Naomi Williams

*"Since we are receiving a Kingdom that is unshakable, let us be thankful and please God by worshiping him with holy fear and awe."*

- Hebrews 12:28 (NLT)

## *Prayer of Gratitude:*
## *Freedom*

Lord today I want to thank You for the freedom in Christ You have given me. Through Christ, You have given me freedom from the sin that so easily entangles me. I have been a prisoner to sin and chained down by heavy weights. Thank You for forgiving me and lifting the weight of my sin off of me.

Thank You for helping me to stand firm in this freedom I have in Christ. Help me not to be burdened again by the regret and shame of my past but empower me to walk in the freedom You have given me. One way I can do this is by putting Your truth, Your Word, into my mind each day. When I know Your truth, it will set me free.

Another way I can stand firm in the freedom You have given me is to come to You daily and confess my sins to You. This keeps me unburdened and free. Bring to my mind any sin I need to confess to You right now. I take this moment to confess these sins to You: _____ (stop and confess your sins to God). Thank You for Your forgiveness. I ask that You empower me to truly change and repent. I love You Lord and I thank You for the freedom You have given me today. Amen.

*"Therefore, since we are surrounded by such a great cloud of witnesses, let us throw off everything that hinders and the sin that so easily entangles. And let us run with perseverance the race marked out for us."*

- Hebrews 12:1

*"It is for freedom that Christ has set us free. Stand firm, then, and do not let yourselves be burdened again by a yoke of slavery."*

- Galatians 5:1 (NIV)

*"Then Jesus said to those Jews who believed Him, "If you abide in My word, you are My disciples indeed. And you shall know the truth, and the truth shall make you free."*

- John 8:31-32

*"Therefore if the Son makes you free, you shall be free indeed."*

- John 8:36

*"The Spirit of the Sovereign Lord is on me, because the Lord has anointed me to proclaim good news to the poor. He has sent me to bind up the brokenhearted, to proclaim freedom for the captives and release from darkness for the prisoners."*

- Isaiah 61:1 (NIV)

## *Story of Gratitude:*
## *In Everything Give Thanks*
### *LaKisha Wheeler*

It was a cold early morning and I was on my way to work. I was definitely not prepared for the day ahead. When I finally arrived to work and got situated, I received a phone call from my supervisor informing me to pack up my things and leave. I was being laid off and didn't see it coming at all. I believe the worse kind of experience anyone can have is when something happens and you are totally not prepared.

Here I was, a single mother of two, driving out of my security into the unknown. As I was driving home and feeling numb, I said a small prayer and I knew that I would find a job in no time. But God had other plans! Days, weeks, and then months went by and nothing. I applied for thousands of jobs and only had two interviews, in which I was not chosen for either job.

During my season of unemployment, I had to move in with my parents. I battled with frustration, depression, suicidal thoughts, anger, and fear! Then one day, God began to speak to me and I started reading his words along with other inspirational books.

There was one scripture that stood out to me the most: 1 Thessalonians 5:16-18 *"Rejoice always, pray continually, give thanks in all circumstances; for this is God's will for you in Christ Jesus."* (NIV)

I slowly began to realize that through my season of unemployment, God continued to supply ALL my needs and I should be grateful for all that he had done! I began to be grateful for having a place to stay, food to eat, a car to drive, friends who loved and encouraged me, family support, two wonderful children, etc. I had all these things but yet complained about what I didn't have.

But as I began to thank God each day for all that he had done, and began writing in my Gratitude Journal, I started to notice doors slowly beginning to open. The phone starting ringing, interviews were being set-up and finally after 14 months, I was blessed with a new career! I truly believe this was a direct result of me showing my gratitude to God for all he had done.

Gratitude shifts your focus from what your life lacks to the abundance that is already present. Everyone has something in their life to feel grateful for. If you can just take time out to think on these things, and to offer thanks to God for the good he has done, then you heal your mind of any negativity which may be affecting you.
Make gratitude a priority in your life; you will be glad you did.

# Day #20:

I thought that today as my 21 day gratitude challenge winds down, I would share several quotes that relate to being thankful and living a life filled with gratitude.

## *The Gratitude Challenge:*

Choose one of the quotes below that impacts you the most and write it out on a notecard or sticky note. Put the quote somewhere where you will see it every day.

*"The unthankful heart discovers no mercies; but the thankful heart will find, in every hour, some heavenly blessings."* - Henry Ward Beecher

*"Gratitude shouldn't be an occasional incident but a continuous attitude."* - Selected

*"The hardest arithmetic to master is that which enables us to count our blessings."* - Eric Hoffer

*"Pride slays thanksgiving, but a humble mind is the soil out of which thanks naturally grows. A proud man is seldom a grateful man, for he never thinks he gets as much as he deserves."* - Henry Ward Beecher

*"We prevent God from giving us the great spiritual gifts He has in store for us, because we do not give thanks for daily gifts. We think we dare not be satisfied with the small measure of spiritual knowledge, experience, and love that has been given to us...We pray for the big things and forget to give thanks for the ordinary, small (and yet really not small) gifts. How can God entrust great things to one who will not thankfully receive from Him the little things?"* - Dietrich Bonhoeffer

*"If you can't be content with what you have received, be thankful for what you have escaped."* - Author unknown

*"God gave you a gift of 86,400 seconds today. Have you used one to say 'thank you'?"* - William A. Ward

*"I thank God for my handicaps, for, through them, I have found myself, my work and my God."* - Helen Keller

## Prayer of Gratitude: Patience

Lord today I want to thank You for patience. Patience is definitely not something that comes naturally to me but is a supernatural gift from Your Spirit. Thank You for equipping me with patience for people and circumstances in my life. Many times, things do not happen the way I plan or in the timing I would like. I surrender my desire to control the people and happenings in my life to You. Help me to have Your patience and contentment even when my circumstances do not change.

Waiting on You is hard. But, ultimately I know that Your timing is best. Give me the ability to see life through Your perspective, an eternal perspective. I want to love others with Your love, a love that is patient and kind. However, I know that I cannot do it on my own strength and that I need Your empowerment to change.

I love You Lord. Even when I am waiting on You and do not see any changes, I trust You with the details of my life. Amen.

*"But the fruit of the Spirit is love, joy, peace, longsuffering, kindness, goodness, faithfulness, gentleness, self-control. Against such there is no law."*
- Galatians 5:22-23

*"Rest in the Lord, and wait patiently for Him."*
- Psalm 37:7a

*"Love is patient, love is kind. It does not envy, it does not boast, it is not proud."*
- I Corinthians 13:4 (NIV)

*"And let us not grow weary while doing good, for in due season we shall reap if we do not lose heart."*
- Galatians 6:9

## *Story of Gratitude:*
## *A Thankful Heart*

*Jennifer Chen*

Not too long ago I went through a lot of trials and tribulations in my life that really tested my faith in Jesus Christ. I have been a Christian for seven years and constantly I go through temptations and seasons of bitterness, anger and hopelessness. At this point in my life I decided to start a clean slate with God and was baptized again to declare my love and devotion to Him. But giving up everything for him was quite hard.

Needless to say, the *21 Days of Gratitude Challenge* couldn't have come at a better time. I feel blessed to have come across this challenge because it has made me grow as a Christian and learn to appreciate so many things more in life that I was taking for granted. I came to realize how lucky I was to have all the things I had and every day going through each exercise made me love the Lord more and others more. It helped me gain more patience for others and show more love towards them.

Writing thank you cards to my loved ones reassured me how blessed I am to have them in my life and that things are worth living for even when it appears hopeless. God used this to let me know that there were people out there who cared about me and that I was not alone. During the 21 days of gratitude, I wrote out what I was thankful for each day. This made me more grateful for the people in my life. For instance, my grandma, who helps me financially once in a while and is always asking me to come over her house to eat. She always takes good care of me. I've also learned to rely on God's strength to pull me through with interviews for jobs and having hope after being out of a job for a long time. I was blessed to have many interviews throughout this time and God keeps providing and showing His amazing grace! I now have an official offer for a job and another interview coming up. God is so great!

We need to remind ourselves that we can truly do all things in Christ who strengthens us (Philippians 4:13) and to always trust in the Lord in all situations and not in our own understanding (Proverbs 3:5-6) and He will make things right. And most important of all, never cease praying and be thankful in all circumstances (1 Thessalonians 5:18) because God does not do evil and whatever happens is according to His will for you.

During this time, I was in the middle of a rocky relationship with my friend and I believe having gratitude towards her helped our relationship to improve and grow. I couldn't have done this without God. We should constantly remind ourselves of His great love for us, how great is He who gave up his only son just to die for OUR sins?! Just so we can be saved. The gratitude challenge helped me marvel in his glory and was a constant reminder of why I am here on Earth and why I do the things I do. I thank God that he gave me the opportunity to work with the kids and teach them about Him. Working with them shows me the millions of blessings that God has put upon me and helps me to complain less and continue to show His love.

What I got most out of the gratitude challenge is that we should be thankful for what we have, not what we don't have, because there are people out there that are in far worse situations than us. We just need to give our problems to God and those problems in comparison to God are really small. God is bigger than any problem we will ever have and if we put our burdens on Him, He will handle it all. We just have to keep having a thankful and grateful heart! I pray that this gratitude challenge will have as great of an impact on everyone who does it as it has had on me. Thank you Shelley and most of all thank you God!

# Day #21:

Wow…it's hard to believe it is day 21 already. Three weeks. It went by so fast and yet God has done a lot of work in my heart over these last 21 days. I know it is just the beginning as a life of gratitude is like a garden…it takes an intentional effort to cultivate. Just like a garden, when we begin to neglect our relationship with Jesus and allow negativity to creep in, it is like weeds growing and choking out the life giving plants. The "weeds" that can grow in our garden of gratitude are self-pity, a complaining spirit, a negative attitude, etc. And if we aren't careful, these "weeds" can soon take over our entire "garden."

However, I have seen God begin to uproot some of these weeds in my heart over the last 21 days and water the life-giving plants in my heart. He has done the work in my heart; it was nothing that I could do on my own through self-help or self-effort.

And as I've surrendered myself to God, confessed my sin of a negative attitude and taken intentional steps to gratitude, some amazing things have happened. We have started to make friends and find community among other believers in a church in our new location.

However, life is not perfect and I still have struggles from day to day. And yet God is helping me to see things from a different perspective.

## Seeing From a Different Perspective

As I was thinking about this yesterday, God immediately brought an illustration to my mind. Have you ever seen optical illusions that look like one thing, but really are another?

I found a couple to share with you. The first is an illusion created by Edward H. Adelson, Professor of Vision Science at MIT. Believe it or not, Box A and Box B are the exact same color in the picture below.

Edward H. Adelson

Source: http://web.mit.edu/persci/people/adelson/checkershadow_illusion.html

Hard to believe, right? But, it's true! I even checked it with my graphics program, Adobe Photoshop, and sure enough each box comes up as the EXACT same color, #787878.

And it reminded me that often times, as followers of Jesus, we look at our circumstances and see our life differently than what is really true. Our enemy, Satan, is the "father of all lies" and many times presents a situation to us that, like the picture above, looks different than it really is. And instead of seeing the truth of how blessed we are or all the spiritual blessings God showers upon us each day, we see only the negative and how we wish things could be different.

It's all a matter of perspective of what we choose to focus on, right? If we are looking for it, we can always see the negative in our lives. However, when looking at the same circumstances we can also see the positive and all that God has given us.

As my 21 day gratitude challenge comes to an end, I pray that God empowers me through His Holy Spirit to continue to see the good in my life and circumstances. And that I continue to cultivate my garden of gratitude each day and not let the weeds overtake it ever again.

## The Gratitude Challenge:

What are you focusing on today in your life? The positive or the negative? I encourage you to focus on all that God has given you today. It's all a matter of perspective.

*"The optimist says, the cup is half full. The pessimist says, the cup is half empty. The child of God says; My cup runneth over."* - Anonymous

*"My [brimming] cup runs over."*

- Psalm 23:5 (AMP)

*"The Lord is my shepherd;*
*I shall not want.*
*He makes me to lie down in green pastures;*
*He leads me beside the still waters.*
*He restores my soul;*
*He leads me in the paths of righteousness*
*For His name's sake.*
*Yea, though I walk through the valley of the shadow of death,*
*I will fear no evil;*
*For You are with me;*
*Your rod and Your staff, they comfort me.*
*You prepare a table before me in the presence of my enemies;*
*You anoint my head with oil;*
***My cup runs over.***
*Surely goodness and mercy shall follow me*
*All the days of my life;*
*And I will dwell in the house of the Lord*
*Forever."*

- Psalm 23

## *Prayer of Gratitude: Salvation*

Lord today I want to thank You for my salvation. I know that without You, I would have no hope beyond this life. For I have sinned against You in so many ways and my sin separates me from You. Thank You that You have given me the gift of eternal life through the sacrifice Jesus made on the cross. So many misunderstand You...You did not send Jesus to condemn the world, but to save it. I pray that my unsaved relatives and friends would come to truly know You and trust in Jesus for their salvation. For when we confess with our mouths that Jesus is Lord and believe in our hearts that You raised him from the dead, we will be saved.

I thank You that salvation is truly a gift from You, nothing I can earn by doing good works or trying harder. Faith without works is dead, but ultimately salvation comes only as a gift from You.

I praise You that I am a new creation – the old has passed away and the new has come. Thank You for changing my heart and my life...I am forever grateful to You. Help me to share my relationship with You with others. Amen.

*"For all have sinned and fall short of the glory of God."*
- Romans 3:23

*"For the wages of sin is death, but the gift of God is eternal life in Christ Jesus our Lord."*
- Romans 6:23

*"For God so loved the world that He gave His only begotten Son, that whoever believes in Him should not perish but have everlasting life. For God did not send His*

*Son into the world to condemn the world, but that the world through Him might be saved."*

- John 3:16-17

*"That if you confess with your mouth the Lord Jesus and believe in your heart that God has raised Him from the dead, you will be saved."*

- Romans 10:9

*"For by grace you have been saved through faith, and that not of yourselves; it is the gift of God."*

- Ephesians 2:8

*"Thus also faith by itself, if it does not have works, is dead."*

- James 2:17

*"Therefore, if anyone is in Christ, he is a new creation; old things have passed away; behold, all things have become new."*

- 2 Corinthians 5:17

## Story of Gratitude:
## Lost But Not Forgotten

*Rob Stephens*

I am only a messenger and witness to share the truth of what God has done in my life that opened my heart with love and gratitude for an awesome God! I was not raised in a Christian home. I lost my father when I was about two years old due to suicide. I was in trouble with the law and going to court since early elementary school as a result of

141

violence and stealing. I was a thief with a major anger problem.

There I was, 21 years old and on the brink of living my life while being in and out of prison. To be honest, I started to believe I was meant for bad things. Scary thought I know, but this is when God carried me out as a result of his grace and mercy! He used a godly man to take me under his wing, opened my heart to accept Christ and brought me out of my own destruction. This was the moment that began my relationship with Jesus and put my life on a path full of thankfulness. Since then, I've been moving forward in his perfect timing.

So there I was, 21 years old. It was 5am and I'd been drinking a lot. I had money in my pocket but decided to get into unlocked cars and look for whatever I could find. I had a no-conscience, nothing-to-lose attitude and was a defiant lost soul! That night I stole a cell phone which at this time consisted of a magnetic antenna that you place on a roof. After stealing the phone, the antenna was sticking straight up over the back of my head through my coat. This had to have been a dead giveaway - ha! I was only about thirty steps away from where I was staying when a policeman spotted and questioned me before he left with the phone, knowing (but couldn't prove) it was stolen until someone called to report it. I stayed awake till later that morning thinking maybe if I go back to the house I could get them to lie for me. It was a desperate move on my part.

I walked to the house to ring the doorbell and a woman in curlers answers the door with the biggest smile on her face. It felt like she was sort of expecting me. Definitely not what I was expecting, knowing I was about to tell her that I just stolen her cell phone! She invites me in and then walks her husband down from upstairs to where I was standing. Paul and Sandy are their names. After a little while I noticed Paul was blind and I realized they were religious. They had no intentions to lie for me so I gave in to telling them my whole life story. I knew whatever I did or said wasn't going to go the way that I deviously planned.

Days went by and Paul and Sandy made frequent stops at the place I lived simply to invite me to church with them. I turned them down in pride over and over, wondering why they were even bothering with me. One day I decided to go with them, feeling like a low-life at first but they made me realize I was accepted as I am. The more I was with them the more I became comfortable with them and myself and I started going with them more often.

Time went by and the time for the court date was here. After the court date I was sitting in jail in an orange jumpsuit which meant felony charges and I wouldn't be going home anytime soon. The court date for sentencing came and Paul somehow convinced the judge and prosecutor that there was still hope for me when even I myself had doubts. My sentence was dropped down to 30 days in jail!

When my 30 days were up I was released to find out Paul had offered me a job at his car dealership and shortly after that invited me to live with him, his wife Sandy and his daughter Christy who at this time was 8 years old. "Wow!" I thought. How can this man invite me to live with him and his family after what I did to them! So I made sure I behaved myself and did whatever he wanted me to do out of respect of his trust in me. I learned so much from just being around a loving family.

Shortly after living with them I decided to turn my life over to Jesus and was baptized. This was my biggest life-changing event and I knew only God could bring about this change within me! I took the first step and then God took over.

I eventually fell to temptation which led me away from Paul and his family after three months of living with them. I even came to the point of suicide not long after this but God wouldn't allow me to take my life.

The fact that I have not stolen anything since that time and that Christ has continued bringing me ever so close to Him gives me a heart so full of thanks and gratitude. And the blessings continue to flow since this was only the beginning of my path towards our awesome God whom we serve.

This is my personal thanks to God...my gratitude for what He has done for me.

*"I give you thanks, O LORD, with all my heart; I will sing your praises before the gods. I bow before your holy Temple as I worship. I praise your name for your unfailing love and faithfulness; for your promises are backed by all the honor of your name. As soon as I pray, you answer me; you encourage me by giving me strength."*
- Psalm 138:1-3 (NLT)

# In Closing...

## *Gratitude in the Midst of Pain*
### *Shelley Hitz*

On January 12, 2010, a 7.0 magnitude earthquake hit Haiti at 4:53pm. It has been reported that 230,000 people died, 300,000 were injured and over 1 million left homeless from this massive earthquake. In just 53 seconds, millions of lives were changed forever. And mine was one of them.

You see, just a month later, on February 11th, I boarded a charter plane as part of a medical relief team to help those who had been injured in the earthquake. I was given this opportunity to use my skills as a Physical Therapist in a small field hospital run by Heartline Ministries. The two weeks I spent in Haiti were a life changing experience for me. Hands down...I will never forget it.

Although I went to Haiti to help these patients, they helped me learn a powerful lesson in gratitude. Every morning as I entered this makeshift hospital, I was greeted by 30+ patients smiling from ear to ear saying, "Bon Jour" or "Shelley!" They were lying in cots that were low to the floor which made transfers and walking very difficult for them. Many of my patients had broken their femur (their thigh bone) in the earthquake and so had a metal external fixator on their leg that they had to carry with them everywhere. It was awkward and heavy, not to mention painful, to transfer with these external fixators. And even though they had to get out of a very low-to-the-ground cot to stand up and walk in therapy, they didn't complain. And most of them had very little pain medication (if any) because our supplies were so limited. I couldn't believe the resilience I encountered.

There is one night during my trip to Haiti that I will never forget. We were finished working for the day and were getting ready to leave for dinner and then to head back to our host homes. Before we left, they asked all of the medical staff to come out into the hospital area. They told us that our patients wanted to thank us for coming to help them and pray for us. Thank us? Really? Wow. Each night they held a church service in this little hospital and tonight they wanted to bless us. Suddenly, they all began to pray at once and many were reaching their hands toward us as they prayed. In Haiti, they speak a French-based creole and so I couldn't fully understand what they were saying as they prayed. However, I did keep hearing the word "*Mesi, Mesi*" over and over which means "*Thank you, Thank you.*"

And as I stood there being blessed by people overflowing with gratitude in some of the worst circumstances I have seen in my life, tears ran down my cheeks…tears of joy and gratitude to have known such amazing people.

There is a Haitian Creole phrase which says, "*Lesowa fe viv.*" This means "*From hope, life.*" And I saw this phrase lived out in my patients so vividly. As they demonstrated their hope in Christ with a heart overflowing with gratitude, I saw life rise up within them. For as George Weinberg said, *"Hope never abandons you; you abandon it."*

I pray that you have been encouraged by reading the stories of gratitude in this book. May you never lose hope. For from a hope in Christ, truly does come life...eternal life.

*"May the God of hope fill you with all joy and peace as you trust in him, so that you may overflow with hope by the power of the Holy Spirit."*
- Romans 15:13 (NIV)

## *More Stories of Gratitude:*

I also wanted to share some stories from those who joined our Facebook group and decided to take the 21 Days of Gratitude Challenge:

***Laurie MacPherson*** - "This gratitude challenge is spreading! Right now my mom and I are talking about gratitude and faith, something she really needs right now. We recently lost my Dad, and it has been hard for us, especially my mama. Now we're having an excellent conversation. This challenge has been quite an inspiration. Keep up the great work. It's contagious! Wow!"

***David Rickey*** - I want to share what this Gratitude Challenge has done for me since I have started. I am on day 13 and I can honestly say this has made me think about every single way I go about life. It has brought to my attention on how much I complain about the tiniest of things when I have such a blessed and fulfilled life. It has also taught me that I have so many things to be thankful for. It has helped me find happiness in life I haven't had in a while.

I think everyone should do this challenge if they haven't yet. You will be blessed.

Another thing this challenge has done is to bring me closer with the big guy upstairs, my true father, my Jesus, my provider, my everything. I feel like since I have started this God and I have started to kindle an intimate relationship with each other that I have never experienced before, it's something that no human or women can ever give me on this earth and it is something that will never be taken from me. All I want to do is draw closer to you God, that is my only desire since I have started this. Bless you everybody and I hope you get as much out of this as I did. :D

*Renee Snyder* - The gratitude challenge has been life changing for me. I usually post in the early part of the day. That helps me to get my mind and heart focused on good things to start the day off well! It has also helped me to identify what I need to talk with the Lord about when I recognize negative thoughts and attitudes I am having. Doing this daily has drawn me closer to the Lord because I am communicating with him more about real heart and thought issues in "real time." In other words, I'm not just overlooking what is going on inside of me and letting my feelings about circumstances rule the day. I was able to realize that my thoughts hold the reins to my feelings. What I think, and what I feel as a result, affects my behavior.

Now I recognize that I can lead my feelings by choosing my thoughts! I was putting the cart (my feelings) before the horse (my thinking) before. I think that's what negativity is. Our feelings ruling our thoughts.

Also, being mindful to be grateful has helped me to hear his voice better. It's like my radio tuner finally found the station. That surprised me a lot. I didn't realize that my bad attitudes had clogged my hearing so much. The other day, I allowed negativity to rule the day and it was so much more obvious that I had lost my peace! This made it easier to change my mind about the way I was dealing with things, ask for the Lord's help, and get back on course! I intend to make this a lifestyle because through experiencing the changes in my life, I understand why the word of God tells us *"For the rest, brethren, whatever is true, whatever is worthy of reverence and is honorable and seemly, whatever is just, whatever is pure, whatever is lovely and lovable, whatever is kind and winsome and gracious, if there is any virtue and excellence, if there is anything worthy of praise, think on and weigh and take account of these things [fix your minds on them]."* Philippians 4:8 (Philippians 4:4-9 is the passage that really locks in the whole idea of gratitude for me).

I am so thankful that the Lord prompted Shelley to share this challenge with all of us! Above all, I praise Jesus for his grace in providing us all a way to be mindful of the thoughts and attitudes of our hearts, and to experience the difference that gratitude makes in our lives!!!! Gratitude opens the door to God's grace, joy, and peace!

*Antonia Faisant* - I really appreciated the Gratitude Challenge because not only was it confirmation concerning what the Lord has been speaking to me about, but it also solidified my need for it. I really enjoyed sharing, but also loved being encouraged by others and the things they were thankful for each day. I really enjoyed the scripture verses and the application. I think my absolute favorite thing was the gratitude board. This is something that I would like to do as well because then it becomes a lifelong discipline.

This challenge has really changes my focus from the negative things in life and to focus on the good. I believe a thankful heart is a happy heart. Proverbs 17:22 says, *"A cheerful heart is good medicine, but a crushed spirit dries up the bones."*

**Join us here:**
**www.bodyandsoulpublishing.com/gratitudegroup**

# About the Authors

## Story of Gratitude Contributors

*Heather Hart* - First and foremost a servant of Christ, Heather is co-author and editor of the "Teen Devotionals... for Girls!" series. She enjoys sharing her faith with others through writing and strives to please Christ in all she does. Heather is happily married to the man of her dreams and lives life as a stay-at-home/work-at-home, mother of four, and housewife. You can connect with her online via her blog, http://authorheatherhart.blogspot.com

*Staci Stallings* - Staci is a #1 Best Selling author who enjoys the lessons God shares with her and through her. She's founded an author's group called Grace & Faith, which shares Christian author's work all across the Internet. She is also the founder of "Christian Kndle" a site dedicated to sharing the love of Christ through the works of Christian authors with the world.

You can see Staci's books at:
http://ebookromancestories.com
Grace & Faith at: http://graceandfaith4u.com
And Christian Kndle at: http://christiankndle.com

*Gwen Ebner* - Gwen is a professor at Winebrenner Seminary in Findlay OH and teaches in the area of counseling, formation and family ministry. She is also an ordained minister and has served in a church setting. She has written several books, Formed Holy in His Image and Turning Off Noise: Tuning In to Healthy Sound and several small articles. Her website is called www.PersonalGrowthForMe.com.

*Suzanne D. Williams* - Suzanne is a native Floridian, wife, mother, photographer, and writer. She is author of both nonfiction and fiction books. She writes a monthly column for Steves-Digicams.com on the subject of digital photography, as well as devotionals and instructional articles for various blogs. She also does graphic design for self-publishing authors.

To learn more about what she's doing visit http://suzanne-williams-photography.blogspot.com or link with her on Facebook at http://www.facebook.com/suzannedwilliamsauthor.

*Naty Matos* – Naty was born in the city of New York. She grew up in the beautiful Island of Puerto Rico and now lives in the city of Atlanta. She holds a Bachelor's Degree in Clinical Psychology with a Minor in Mass Media Communications and a Master's Degree in Mental Health Counseling.

Naty writes Christian fiction and non-fiction. She maintains a blog on Christian Living Topics at www.therisingmuse.com.

*Janet Perez Eckles* - Although blind, Janet has been inspiring thousands to see the best of life. Her stories, told with a Latina flair and touch of humor, ignite a passion to conquer fear through Christ. She draws insights from her writing found in 28 books, in her keynote messages, and from her recent No. 1 bestselling, inspirational book, Simply Salsa: Dancing Without Fear at God's Fiesta.

When Janet shares the details of losing her sight at 31 and her ability to see the best of life, it will empower you to see the way out of your own difficulties. As you listen to her encounter with marital infidelity, it will show you the path to restoring a marriage by gaining respect, confidence, and dignity. When she shares the healing of the heartache of her youngest son's murder, it will inspire you to overcome tragedy and bring back peace and contentment. And the acquittal of the man responsible will show you how to live in the freedom that forgiveness brings. Janet's achievement as an award-winning Spanish interpreter in spite of her blindness will show you the path to overcome obstacles and soar to success.

Find out more about Janet at her website: www.JanetPerezEckles.com.

*Lorilyn Roberts* – Lorilyn is a Christian author who writes children's picture books, nonfiction, memoirs, and a young adult fantasy series, Seventh Dimension. To learn more about Lorilyn, visit her website at http://lorilynroberts.com To connect with her personally, you can contact her by email at llwroberts at cox.net.

*Alberta Sequeira* – Alberta is an Awareness Coach, producer, director and co-host to the NBTV-95 Cable TV, co-founder to Authors Without Borders.

She is also a four-time award winning author with her three memoirs, A Spiritual Renewal; A Journey to Medjugorje, Someone Stop This Merry-Go-Round; An Alcoholic Family in Crisis and its sequel Please, God, Not Two; This Killer Called Alcoholism.

You can find out more about Alberta or her books at her website www.albertasequeira.com or her blog: www.albertasequeira.wordpress.com.

*Lucille Richardson* – Lucille was born into a family of nineteen children, all having the same mom and dad. She recently celebrated her 87th birthday and is grateful for the long life God has given her. She loves to read and enjoys reading her kindle almost every day. She also enjoys gardening and at one time cared for a big vegetable garden as well as numerous flowers. She has a 'green thumb' and still lovingly cares for her flowers today. She also has an artistic flair and enjoys playing cards and spending time with her family.

*Lucille's story was edited with the help of her daughter, Gwen Ebner.*

*CJ Hitz* - CJ is an author, speaker and entrepreneur. In his downtime, he enjoys spending time outdoors running, hiking and exploring God's beautiful creation. He can be found at www.ChristianSpeakers.tv and www.BodyAndSoulPublishing.com

*Shelley Hitz* – Shelley has been writing and publishing books since 2008. She is also the author of the website, FindYourTrueBeauty.com, that reaches thousands of girls each month around the world. Her openness and vulnerability as she shares her own story of hope and healing will inspire and encourage you.

Shelley has been ministering to teens since 1998 alongside her husband, CJ. They currently travel and speak to teens and adults around the country. Shelley's main passion is to share God's truth and the freedom in Christ she has found with others. She does this through her books, websites and speaking engagements.

You can find more about Shelley at www.ShelleyHitz.com or invite her to speak at your event here: www.ChristianSpeakers.tv.

*Troy Lewis* - Troy is a recent walking miracle, speaker, and author of Another Second Chance. He resides in Northwest Ohio with his lovely wife Stephanie and two beautiful daughters. To learn more about Troy, his story, or to have him share God's Story at your church or event, go to www.another2ndchance.org

*Phyllis Sather* - Phyllis is a wife, mother, and author. She retired from a management position to become a stay at home mom which lead to homeschooling, home college, and home businesses. She is passionate about family life, parenting, homeschooling, writing and her Lord and Savior Jesus Christ. You can purchase her books at www.Phyllis-Sather.com

*Sheri Ketner* - Sheri lives on the Gulf coast of Florida with her husband Keith. Formally a Christian TV producer and the Host of "Grace For Today" enjoys encouraging women to continue in the joy that only God can give as we are faced with everyday issues.

*Kimberly Rae* - Kimberly is the Amazon Bestselling Author of the Stolen Series on international human trafficking and missions (www.stolenwoman.org). She is currently working on a series of books on chronic health issues. Read Kimberly's real-life adventures on her blog, www.stolenwoman.blogspot.com, or contact her through Facebook (Human Trafficking Stolen Woman) or Twitter (KimberlyRae10).

*Kathryn Holmes* - Kathryn is retired. She lives in Minnetonka, Minnesota with her husband, Charlie. Her book, "I Stand With Courage: One Woman's Journey to Conquer Paralysis," is a story of courage, determination, and faith. By sharing her story through her book and speaking to local audiences she has inspired many with her message of hope. Find out more about Kathryn here: www.IStandWithCourage.com.

*LaKisha Wheeler* - LaKisha is a single mother of two wonderful children. LaKisha came to know Christ at the dear age of 14 and throughout the years, she has grown to love God more and more. She is very active in her church and she enjoys reading traveling and helping others. Her motto in life is "No matter what, never, ever, ever, give up". LaKisha resides in Columbia, SC along with her two children.

*Jennifer Chen* - Jennifer describes herself as a friendly person who loves God and loves kids! She has never experienced as great of a love as God's love ever and denying herself and taking up the cross and believing in our Lord Jesus Christ was the best decision she has ever made. She wants to make a difference in this world and will stop at nothing to help others and serve and keep sharing the gospel. Her favorite bible verse is Philippians 4:11-13 because she has been through plenty and little and in the end she has learned to be content no matter what.

# Get Free Christian Books

Love getting FREE Christian books online? If so, sign up to get notified of new Christian book promotions and never miss out. Then, grab a cup of coffee and enjoy reading the free Christian books you download.

You will also get our FREE report, *"How to Find Free Christian Books Online"* that shows you 7 places you can get new books…for free!

Sign up here:  www.bodyandsoulpublishing.com/freebooks

Happy reading!

# CJ and Shelley Hitz

C.J. and Shelley Hitz enjoy sharing God's Truth through their speaking engagements and their writing. On downtime, they enjoy spending time outdoors running, hiking and exploring God's beautiful creation.

To find out more about their ministry or to invite them to your next event, check out their website at: www.ChristianSpeakers.tv

# Other Books by CJ and Shelley Hitz

Forgiveness Formula

Unshackled and Free

Finding Hope in the Midst of Tragedy

Mirror Mirror... Am I Beautiful?

Teen Devotionals... for Girls!

Fuel for the Soul

48733479R10093

Made in the USA
San Bernardino, CA
04 May 2017